ROMANCE MONOGRAPHS, INC.

Number 16

DARKNESS AND LIGHT

LECTURES ON BAUDELAIRE, FLAUBERT, NERVAL,
HUYSMANS, RACINE,

AND

TIME AND ITS IMAGES IN LITERATURE

ROMANCE MONOGRAPHS, INC.

Number 16

DARKNESS AND LIGHT

LECTURES ON BAUDELAIRE, FLAUBERT, NERVAL, HUYSMANS, RACINE,

AND

TIME AND ITS IMAGES IN LITERATURE

BY

ALFRED GARVIN ENGSTROM

ALUMNI DISTINGUISHED PROFESSOR OF FRENCH

IN THE

UNIVERSITY OF NORTH CAROLINA AT CHAPEL HILL

BEING THE FIRST SERIES OF HUMANITIES LECTURES

FOR THE

LIBERAL ARTS FORUM OF ELON COLLEGE

1967-1969

UNIVERSITY, MISSISSIPPI

ROMANCE MONOGRAPHS, INC.

1 9 7 5

Library of Congress Cataloging in Publication Data

Engstrom, Alfred G   1907-
    Darkness and light.

    (Romance monographs; no. 16)

    1. French literature—History and criticism—Addresses, essays, lectures.
2. Time in literature. I. Elon College Liberal Arts Forum. II. Title.

PQ139.E6   840'.9'38   75-20433

For Mary Claire

THE ELON COLLEGE LIBERAL ARTS FORUM

In 1966 when the idea of the Humanities Lectures was conceived, the decision to offer the first lectureship to Alfred Garvin Engstrom was uniformly enthusiastic. The Elon College Liberal Arts Forum, which was to sponsor the series of lectures, had known Professor Engstrom for some years. The membership of the Forum, comprised exclusively of students, was persuaded that he, more than anyone, had been responsible for the extraordinary success which this unique student-operated and student-financed lecture society had enjoyed.

There were to be six lectures in the series, delivered over a period of three years. Professor Engstrom, with characteristic good grace, agreed to the arrangement. In the spring of 1969, during the Forum's annual Symposium, "Studies in the Humanities," the last of the lectures was delivered. On that occasion the Forum, in gratitude for Professor Engstrom's contributions to the academic life of Elon College, established in his honor and in honor of his lovely wife a permanent lectureship, The Alfred Garvin and Mary Claire Engstrom Lecture in Literature. Since then, a scholar of international stature has been invited annually to Elon College to deliver the Engstrom Lecture.

The long and happy association between the Liberal Arts Forum and Professor Engstrom has been an association of kindred spirits. During the difficult years of the late 1960's when issues of war and race brought turbulence to the bucolic campuses of America, the dedication of the Forum to its tradition of humanistic and scholarly programs remained steadfast. In maintaining faith with this lofty commitment, students on the Forum helped to shed reason and light in a world which was then largely bereft of it. In resisting the popular clamor for the noisy and profane, they exhibited profound good judgement and an independence almost unique among their contemporaries. But above all else, what separated and distinguished the Forum from other college lecture societies was the thoughtful, courteous attention which the student members devoted to every guest. In this the Forum was joined by a host of townspeople who generously extended the hospitality of their gracious homes to assure that the occasion of every lecture was a memorable and meaningful experience. The Forum's national recognition was ultimately a consequence of the collective enterprise of students, townspeople and of course guest lecturers such as Alfred Engstrom. As the only faculty advisor whom the students on the Forum knew for nearly a decade, my regard for their estimable services and my affection for them personally is unbounded.

Professor Engstrom's career as a distinguished teacher and scholar over four decades at the University of North Carolina at Chapel Hill has earned for him the respect and love of legions of students and colleagues. That these sentiments are shared at Elon College goes unquestioned. The publication of this first series of Humanities Lectures reflects the abiding admiration which the Liberal Arts Forum holds for him. This wonderfully witty, considerate and learned man has been both companion and inspiration to hundreds of students at Elon College. To all those who have known him, he has been a model of civility and learning, of kindliness and humanity, which could serve as example for a greater part of the human community.

JAMES P. ELDER, JR.
Folger Shakespeare Library
Washington, D.C.
(formerly of Elon College)

CONTENTS

I

CHARLES BAUDELAIRE (1821-1867) AND THE ALCHEMY OF *LES FLEURS DU MAL*

THE PRESENT YEAR marks the hundredth anniversary of the death of Charles Baudelaire, the author of *Les Fleurs du Mal,* one of the most influential and most memorable volumes of poetry in the modern world. It is a book I never open without a sense of anticipation and wonder, for it contains poems of remarkable power, strangeness and complex beauty, and one never knows quite what will appear in them as he reads.

Baudelaire himself insisted that for a work of art to have lasting interest it must be animated by what we may term the accent of its time. In *Les Fleurs du Mal* the accent is from mid-nineteenth-century Paris; but it is the accent of an observer who, while looking with deep understanding upon many aspects of human suffering, has looked at the same time with loathing upon the mores and tastes and admirations of the prevailing society.

It is one of the supreme ironies of the period that Baudelaire and Flaubert, two of the century's greatest writers, were haled into court, and in the same year (1857), on charges that their finest works *(Les Fleurs du Mal* and *Madame Bovary),* which had just appeared, were offensive to religion and to public morality and decency. Flaubert was declared innocent of such offenses; but Baudelaire and his publishers, though acquitted of the charge of offenses against religion, were found guilty of offending public morality and decency and were sentenced to pay fines and to delete six poems from *Les Fleurs du Mal.*

This was a bitter affront and humiliation; but the irony of such a trial and its outcome must have had a certain acrid savor for so critical an intelligence as Baudelaire, whose opinion of his accusers may be imagined from a passage in the part of his *Intimate Journals* called *Fusées (Skyrockets):* "If a poet requested from the State the right to have a few bourgeois in his stable, people would be thunderstruck, whereas if a bourgeois called for roast poet it would be considered perfectly natural."

For Baudelaire, the contemporary materialism and its attendant belief in progress were utterly antipathetic. He had no faith in the current ideas for human betterment and held very gloomy views as to the essential nature of man: "Whether man snares his victim on the boulevard, or spears his prey in trackless forests, is he not eternal man, that is to say the most perfect beast of prey?" As for the idea of progress itself, Baudelaire found this "a doctrine of idlers . . . the individual counting on his neighbors to do his task." In *Mon cœur mis à nu (My Heart Laid Bare),* the second part of his *Intimate Journals* with a title adopted from Edgar Allan Poe, he writes that true civilization is not in gas or steam or table-turnings but "in the diminution of the traces of original sin."

Like the *grands classiques* of the seventeenth century, whom he resembles in many ways, Baudelaire was thus concerned primarily with the inner life of man — with the moral, religious, psychological and aesthetic aspects of human experience. His own background was Catholic and, even though we cannot with any assurance identify him as a practicing member of the faith, his thought is in many respects essentially Christian and he seems, in certain ways, much closer to Augustine than to most of the representative thinkers of his time. In a sense, he may be called an Augustinian with only the faintest of hopes for salvation — and this is a very bleak characterization indeed; but he kept the dimension of eternity in his spiritual view of man, and he seems to me, in spite of the ambiguous conclusion of *Les Fleurs du Mal,* to deserve identification as one of the last great Christian poets up to our day.

This evening, in the centennial year of Baudelaire's death, I hope to bring before you some sense of his remarkable qualities and of his pertinence for our time, and to show at least something of the enduring beauty and the vision of the modern world that he left us from a life of suffering in the volume of poems which he called by the strange and provocative title, *Les Fleurs du Mal.*

I

The first edition of Baudelaire's famous book in 1857 contained only a hundred poems, and one of the finest divisions of the later collection, the part called "Tableaux Parisiens" or "Parisian Scenes," was not included, although eight of its eighteen poems appeared in other parts of the volume. The third edition, of 1868, was put in order by friends after the poet's death and is of little use for studying the form of the work, though it contains a few beautiful poems not included with the earlier texts. Our examination tonight will be concerned, then, largely with the second edition — the edition of 1861 — whose "architecture," as it has been called, was the latest form of the volume to be shaped and arranged by Baudelaire's own hand.

* * *

Les Fleurs du Mal! Even today, after long acquaintance with the poetry of Baudelaire, when I see the famous title I am puzzled as to how it can be adequately rendered into English. *Flowers of Evil* once seemed a simple and clear and precise translation; but I find these words now so lacking in the rich semantic echoes and interplays to be found in the French and so misleading in their single emphasis that they no longer seem to me valid equivalents.

There has, in fact, been a long controversy over Baudelaire's title, and I suspect that this, too, has arisen in part from a failure to recognize the richness and irony and humanity in his use of the words *Fleurs du Mal.* Thibaudet, a fine and sensitive critic, once wrote that surely the most fanatical champion of Baudelaire would hardly defend what Thibaudet called his "ridiculous and rococo title." Other critics have cited the statement by one of Baudelaire's friends that the title was not even his creation, but was suggested by Hippolyte Babou. Yet, whatever its origin, Baudelaire chose *Les Fleurs du Mal* as the title for his masterpiece; and its pertinence to his poems can, in my judgment, not only be demonstrated, but can serve to show that the whole volume deserves to be considered from a more diversified viewpoint than that entailed in seeing the poems under the unique focus of *Flowers of Evil.*

We shall see hereafter examples of flowers in Baudelaire's verses; but it is worth noting that overt and implied flower imagery is evident in a remarkable number of the poems, that there is in the volume a continuing sense of natural ripening, flowering and fading of flowers and other vegetation, and that Baudelaire on a number of occasions specifically refers to poems as flowers. It was the ironic combination of such a word as *Fleurs* (with its connotations of beauty and purity and innocence, as well as of quintessence) with the word *Mal,* taken in the sense of *Evil,* that furnished much of the provocative shock in the title *Les Fleurs du Mal,* conceived precisely even by the French as *Flowers of Evil.*

But the word *mal* does not mean only *evil* in the moral and theological sense, as it seems most often to have been uniquely understood and translated in Baudelaire's title. The first definition of *le mal* in Littré's great dictionary in 1873 is "ce qui nuit, ce qui blesse; le contraire du bien" ("what harms or hurts; the opposite of *le bien*"); and thereafter, along with the sense of moral and metaphysical *evil,* the word is given the definition of "les souffrances, les maladies, la mort" ("sufferings, diseases, death"). So there is a richer sense to *Les Fleurs du Mal* than merely *Flowers of Evil,* however pertinent this title may be to a pervading atmosphere in the book and to many of its poems. The word *mal* must be seen here to include the sense of *suffering* of all kinds and *misfortune* and *death,* along with the sense of moral and metaphysical *evil* — and *Les Fleurs du Mal* thus becomes, in addition to *Flowers of Evil,* Flowers of any of the myriad forms of human Suffering (that is, Flowers of *Boredom* and *Illness* and *Despair* and *Loneliness* and *Humiliation* and *Degradation* and *Remorse* and *Regret* and the *Fear of Passing Time* and the like) and Flowers of *Death* — a long trail of Baudelaire's major themes in *Les Fleurs du Mal.* All this seems to me to entail a broader sense of humanity than that implied in restricting the sense of *mal* to *evil* in the title of the poems.

According to Baudelaire, *Les Fleurs du Mal* "must be judged as a whole, and then there emerges from it a terrible morality." Later, after his trial, he wrote of the volume: ". . . into this *atrocious* book I have put *my whole heart, all my love, all my religion* (disguised), *all my hatred.*" Beyond all else it seems to have been through *Les Fleurs du Mal* that Baudelaire gave meaning to his life, and in turning now to the collection itself we shall try to show something of the poet's thought and the alchemy of his art in the poems of his masterpiece.

The dedication of *Les Fleurs du Mal* to Théophile Gautier is of unusual interest, not only for its homage to a gifted poet and friend, but for certain revelations as to Baudelaire's own conception of the poet's art. The dedication is phrased as follows:

> To the impeccable poet
> To the perfect magician in French letters
> To my very dear and very revered
> Master and friend
> Théophile Gautier
> with feelings
> of the most profound humility
> I dedicate
> these sickly flowers.
> C. B.

In the phrase "impeccable poet" Baudelaire pays homage to exquisite form — to the poet as artist and craftsman; and Baudelaire's own influence continues this tradition of the poet, which he drew in part from Gautier and, in a somewhat different sense, from Poe and passed on to Mallarmé and Valéry. The phrase "perfect magician," on the other hand, implies a very different conception of poetry; and here we sense the idea of the poet as mage or seer that Baudelaire was to transmit to Rimbaud and his followers. Finally, in the phrase "sickly flowers" for his poems we see clear evidence in the very dedication to his work that the *Fleurs du Mal* were not seen by the poet only as flowers of moral and theological evil.

Of even greater interest than the dedication is the introductory poem, "Au lecteur" ("To the Reader"), which serves as a preface to the whole collection. This is a scathing denunciation of the age in which it was written, but it shows at the same time the poet's own harrowing metaphysical and religious preoccupations and his despair at the hopelessness of the human situation. The brilliant and unexpected imagery in the poem's forty verses creates an unforgettable atmosphere of evil and human degradation and provides a strange and terrible entry into the remarkable world of Baudelaire's poetry.

The first word in "Au lecteur" (and thus the first word in *Les Fleurs du Mal*) is *sottise* (stupidity), a quality that Baudelaire loathed as deeply as Flaubert; and the poem's last verse is one of the most famous satiric lines in modern literature: "—Hypocrite lecteur, —mon semblable, —mon frère!" ("Hypocritical reader, —my fellowman, —my brother!") Here Baudelaire was not flattering the "gentle reader" of polite society. He was flaying his age. Perhaps not since Dante created his Vestibule for the trimmers, who were not even worthy of Hell, has there been so cruel a representation of mediocrity as in this prefatory poem.

Like Dante, Baudelaire uses vulgar imagery for vulgar characterizations; but his art, like Dante's, transforms the vulgar into powerful, imaginative creation. He describes contemporary man's mind and body as occupied and shaped by "stupidity, error, sin, and stinginess" (this last a base fault, lacking the intensity and magnitude of avarice); and he adds:

> Et nous alimentons nos aimables remords
> Comme les mendiants nourissent leur vermine.
>
> [And we nourish our charming remorse
> As beggars nourish their vermine.]

Here the brilliance of the language centers on the word *remords* (in the plural) and its etymology and its relationship with other words in the poem, so that unless one thinks of the root meaning of *remorse* the power of the imagery is lost.

In its true sense, *remorse* is a "biting back" — a cruel self-devouring. Remorse is so fearful a state that we have, in warning against it, a famous Greek adage attributed to Pythagoras: "Eat not the heart." But in Baudelaire's indictment of his age *remorse* is attractive and man is seen nourishing his remorse "as beggars nourish their vermine." Thus the deep bite of true remorse has given way to something that can be equated with the vulgar and superficial irritations of a beggar's lice; and the beggar imagery itself suggests a further degradation in man's superficially begging forgiveness for his sins. Baudelaire continues his indictment with cruel insistence:

Nos péchés sont têtus, nos repentirs sont lâches;
Nous nous faisons payer grassement nos aveux,
Et nous rentrons gaiement dans le chemin bourbeux,
Croyant par de vils pleurs laver toutes nos taches.

[Our sins are headstrong, our repentances base;
We arrange to be well paid for our confessions,
And we return gaily into the muddy way,
Thinking by vile tears to wash clean all our stains.]

Here the poet introduces the first of his great images of Satan, whom he calls Satan Trismégiste (Satan Trismegistus — Thrice-Powerful Satan) and thus establishes a relation with Hermes Trismegistus, the supposed author of esoteric books on magic and alchemy. This is one of the most dramatic appearances of Satan in all the writings of Baudelaire, where his presence is so often felt.

Sur l'oreiller du mal c'est Satan Trismégiste
Qui berce longuement notre esprit enchanté,
Et le riche métal de notre volonté
Est tout vaporisé par ce savant chimiste.

[On the pillow of evil [i.e., Sloth, one of the Seven Deadly
    Sins] it is Satan Trismegistus
Who lulls for a long while our enchanted spirit,
And the rich metal of our will
Is all vaporized by this learned chemist.]

In his book on opium and hashish called *The Artificial Paradises,* Baudelaire refers to the will as "the most precious of all the faculties" and as "cette précieuse *substance*" ("this precious *substance*"). Thus Satan is seen as a diabolical alchemist who, instead of transforming the baser metals into gold, vaporizes the most precious gold of the will as man lies enthralled to Sloth.

Once his will is dissolved, man is an easy prey; and the next stanza of the poem introduces the Devil as the great puppet-master, pulling the threads that govern human actions, until man without horror goes down each day one further step towards Hell, while demons carouse in his brain and Death descends into his lungs like an invisible stream. In this weird puppet-show, if man is not guilty of rape and poisoning and stabbing and setting fire to things around him, it is not from his native virtue — "It is because our soul, alas! is not bold enough."

Baudelaire writes in a letter of 1856 that he has often thought that this world's maleficent and disgusting animals "were perhaps only the vivification, the corporification, the flowering, in material life, of man's evil thoughts." And he adds: "Thus all *nature* participates in original sin." And so in "Au lecteur" he imagines seven yelping, howling, crawling monsters in what he calls "the infamous menagerie of our vices" — and he adds an eighth that will make its presence felt thereafter as one of the most terrible forces in *Les Fleurs du Mal.* In addition to the seven monsters, then . . .

> Il en est un plus laid, plus méchant, plus immonde!
> Quoiqu'il ne pousse ni grands gestes ni grands cris,
> Il ferait volontiers de la terre un débris
> Et dans un bâillement avalerait le monde;
>
> C'est l'Ennui! —l'œil chargé d'un pleur involontaire,
> Il rêve d'échafauds en fumant son houka.
> Tu le connais, lecteur, ce monstre délicat,
> —Hypocrite lecteur, —mon semblable, —mon frère!
>
> [There is one more ugly, more wicked, more foul!
> Although he makes no great motions or cries,
> He would willingly reduce the earth to ruin
> And in one yawn swallow all the world.
>
> He is ENNUI! —His eye laden with an involuntary tear,
> He dreams of scaffolds as he smokes his houka.
> You know him, reader, this delicate monster,
> —Hypocritical reader, —my fellowman, —my brother!]

Ennui, the "delicate monster," a nineteenth-century equivalent of the deadly sin of Sloth or Tristitia or *taedium vitae* or *acedia,* which he called "the malady of monks," will pursue Baudelaire all the rest of his life.

II

Apart from the verses "To the Reader," the 1861 edition of *Les Fleurs du Mal* has 126 poems grouped in six unequal divisions called in turn *Spleen and Ideal, Parisian Scenes, Wine, Fleurs du Mal, Revolt,* and *Death.* For our purposes this evening, however, I have decided to consider Baudelaire's poems under certain selected headings that seem to afford especially pertinent insights into his art. We shall thus examine first of all in some detail Baudelaire's rather complex and perverse aesthetic ideas as shown in certain of his poems on beauty. Thereafter we shall consider briefly in turn his treatment of sin and love and woman; of spleen or ennui; of the sea and voyages; and of Death. Finally, at the last, in order to see something of the poet's own ordering and imaginative creation and shaping of materials on a concentrated subject, we shall consider the poems in the division of *Les Fleurs du Mal* called "Tableaux Parisiens" ("Parisian Scenes"), Baudelaire's remarkable evocation of the human dramas and the spiritual and moral forces at work in one of the great capitals of modern Europe — what he himself called, as we shall see hereafter, "the heroism of modern life."

* * *

Baudelaire writes in the part of his *Intimate Journals* called *My Heart Laid Bare* that even in childhood he had felt "two contradictory sentiments, the horror of life and the ecstasy of life"; and he notes that "there are in every man, at every hour, two simultaneous postulations, one towards God and the other towards Satan" . . . the spiritual and the animal. In the representations of Beauty in *Les Fleurs du Mal* we find interplay of comparable dualities, as is evident from an examination of such poems in *Spleen and Ideal* as "Correspondences," "The Lighthouses," "Beauty," "The Ideal," and "Hymn to Beauty" — five poems that deserve special consideration for their summary of much of Baudelaire's aesthetics and for the rich insights they give us into the imagination of a great poet who defined the study of the beautiful as "a duel in which the artist cries out in terror before being conquered" ("Le confiteor de l'artiste").

In "Correspondences," the first of these poems, Baudelaire sees Nature as a temple with living pillars from which confused words come forth. Man passes there through "forests of symbols" that look upon him as if there were some intimate relation between him and them. This conception of correspondence between material objects in nature and spiritual, human realities is apparently drawn from Swedenborg. Here Baudelaire develops a second kind of correspondence in his description of the interrelation of sense-perceptions, or what is known as synaesthesia — the metaphor of the senses. This is a phenomenon recurrent in western literature from the *Iliad* to the present day; but it was so consciously employed as a part of late nineteenth-century aesthetics in France that Baudelaire's proclamation of it is of special interest when he writes:

Comme de longs échos qui de loin se confondent
Dans une ténébreuse et profonde unité,
Vaste comme la nuit et comme la clarté,
Les parfums, les couleurs et les sons se répondent.
Il est des parfums frais comme des chairs d'enfants,
Doux comme les hautbois, verts comme les prairies,
—Et d'autres, corrompus, riches et triomphants,
Ayant l'expansion des choses infinies,
Comme l'ambre, le musc, le benjoin et l'encens,
Qui chantent les transports de l'esprit et des sens.

[Like long echoes which from far away are fused
In a shadowy and deep oneness,
Vast as night and as light,
Perfumes, colors and sounds correspond.
There are fragrances cool as children's flesh,
Sweet as oboes, green as prairies,
—And others, tainted, rich and triumphant,
Having the expansiveness of infinite things,
Like ambergris, musk, benzoin and incense
That sing the ecstasies of the spirit and the senses.]

Here we have not only a complex and fascinating relationship between physical objects and spiritual realities, and between the different senses, but also a subtle relationship between these two different kinds of correspondences arranged in a recurrent chiastic pattern that seems to me of special interest.

Critics have suggested that the Swedenborgian correspondences in the poem are "vertical" and that the correspondences between the senses are "horizontal"; and I take this to imply that there is a loftier value given to the first than to the second kind of correspondences. But the chiastic patterns in syntax here suggest that the two different sorts of correspondence combine in a transcendent relationship for the creation of beauty.

Baudelaire cites, for example, as we have seen, fragrances "having the expansiveness of infinite things" — and these are identified as being "like ambergris, musk, benzoin and incense," of which the first two are animal secretions used as a base in sensual perfumes, and the last two are aromatic resins, gums or spices employed in church ritual. But the next verse says that these four fragrances "sing the ecstasy of the spirit and the senses" — and here the pattern of the sensual and the spiritual is reversed so that (in the chiastic relationship) ambergris and musk are counterbalanced by the spirit, and benzoin and incense by the senses. This is a recurrent kind of pattern in Baudelaire, and it seems to me here to imply his belief that interplay with the senses is essential in poetry for the representation of the spiritual. The fact that the perfumes "having the expansiveness of infinite things" are called *corrompus* (tainted) is a jarring note; but, as will be more evident hereafter, Baudelaire includes elements of this sort in his conception of ideal beauty. For Baudelaire, the shadow of original sin apparently falls as darkly over the aesthetic world as over the moral and spiritual worlds.

In a second poem, "The Lighthouses," great works of art are seen as "maledictions, blasphemies, and complaints" — but also as "ecstasies, cries, tears and Te Deums." They are lighthouses "lighted on a thousand citadels," the best witness that man can give of his worth — "[a] burning sob that rolls from age to age and comes to die at the edge of [God's] eternity." Thus Baudelaire recognizes the ephemeral quality of even the greatest art and, though he sees it as witness of what is best in man, he does not confuse art with religion in the dimension of eternity.

The poem called "Beauty" has been interpreted in Thomistic terms, as if it were written under the influence of St. Thomas's statement that, "since God (the noblest of beings) is motionless, in the absolute, immobility is nobler than motion." This sonnet is so memorable a statement of one aspect of Baudelaire's aesthetics that it deserves to be cited as nearly as it can be translated for our purposes. Here Beauty speaks in her own voice:

> I am fair, O mortals! as a dream in stone,
> And my breast, where each one is bruised in turn,
> Is made to inspire in the poet a love
> Eternal and mute as matter.

> I am throned in the azure like an uncomprehended sphinx;
> I unite a heart of snow with the whiteness of swans;
> I hate motion that displaces lines,
> And I never weep and I never laugh.
>
> The poets, before my grand attitudes,
> That I seem to borrow from the proudest monuments,
> Will consume their days in austere studies;
>
> For, to fascinate these docile lovers, I have
> Pure mirrors that make all things more fair;
> My eyes, my wide eyes with their eternal lights!

The eyes of *Les Fleurs du Mal* are unforgettable reflectors of human moods and sorrows and despairs; but here the wide eyes of Beauty open suddenly to show us lights that are eternal.

In the poem called "The Ideal" a more perverse conception of beauty is presented — and it is clearly related to Baudelaire's discussion of his ideal beauty in the *Skyrockets* of his *Intimate Journals,* where he writes:

> I have found the definition of the Beautiful, — of what is for me the Beautiful. It is something ardent and sad, something a little vague, leaving room for conjecture.

Applying these ideas to a woman's beautiful and seductive head, Baudelaire describes it as

> . . . a head that makes one dream at the same time — though confusedly — of voluptuous happiness and of sadness; that admits of an idea of melancholy, of lassitude, even of satiety, — or a contrary idea, that is, an ardor, a desire to be alive, associated with a countercurrent of bitterness, as if coming from deprivation or despair. Mystery and regret are also characteristics of the Beautiful.

As for masculine beauty, Baudelaire would find it hard not to conclude "that the most perfect type of virile Beauty is *Satan,* — as Milton saw him."

Thus, in the poem called "The Ideal," when Baudelaire discusses the ideal woman who would satisfy a heart like his, he finds little charm in what he calls the "hospital beauties" of the women in Gavarni's drawings, and he adds (with remarkable imagery):

> For I cannot find among these pale roses
> One flower that resembles my red ideal.

The first stanza in the sestet of the sonnet is of special interest here:

> What this heart, deep as an abyss, needs
> Is you, Lady Macbeth, soul powerful in crime,
> Dream of Aeschylus thas has opened [like a flower]
>   in a region of storms.

Here the contrast between the flower of his "red ideal" and the "pale roses" of Gavarni's sickly women is heightened when the poet cites his ideal as Lady Macbeth, a "dream of Aeschylus." This clearly links Lady Macbeth with Clytemnestra, and the two murderesses serve to identify the red in the flower of the Ideal as the color of blood.

In "Hymn to Beauty," Baudelaire develops similar ideas in his conception of Beauty as having a glance both infernal and divine, as being comparable to wine in her good and bad effects, and as being omnipotent and responsible to nothing. Does Beauty come down from deep heaven or up from the abyss? Baudelaire pretends not to care, and notes that Horror is not the least charming of her jewels and that Murder, among her most precious trinkets, dances amorously on her proud belly. The concluding stanzas of the poem sum up a despairing aspect of the function of Beauty in this world:

> Que tu viennes du ciel ou de l'enfer, qu'importe,
> O Beauté, monstre énorme, effrayant, ingénu!
> Si ton œil, ton souris, ton pied, m'ouvrent la porte
> D'un Infini que j'aime et n'ai jamais connu?
>
> De Satan ou de Dieu, qu'importe? Ange ou Sirène,
> Qu'importe, si tu rends, —fée aux yeux de velours,
> Rhythme, parfum, lueur, ô mon unique reine!—
> L'univers moins hideux et les instants moins lourds?
>
> [What matter whether you come from heaven or hell, —
> O Beauty! enormous, terryfying, ingenuous monster!
> If your eye, your smile, your foot, open for me the door
> Of an Infinite I love and have never known?
>
> From Satan or from God, what matter? Angel or Siren,
> What matter — fay with the velvet eyes,

Rhythm, perfume, light, O my only queen! —
If you make the universe less hideous and the moments less dull?]

The poet seems here at the last to define the ultimate function of beauty as being merely to help make endurable the terrible boredom of human life. But he suggests that this may be accomplished by her opening a door on the Infinite.

In the consideration of five poems from *Spleen and Ideal* we have thus seen how Baudelaire, in his search for beauty, urged the use of correspondences in both the Swedenborgian and synaesthetic senses — the concept of art as proof of man's essential worth — the idea of the remoteness and austerity of Beauty — the recognition that in human beauty there can be sinister qualities like those in Lady Macbeth and Clytemnestra, and in Satan as Milton saw him — and a belief that such elements as horror and murder can be adornments of Beauty when man seeks it to relieve the boredom of existence and to open a door on the infinite. Here, amidst the strange and perverse elements in Baudelaire's aesthetics, there is still the notion of eternity (Beauty's eyes with their eternal lights, and "an Infinite I love and have never known"); but it may be seen, as we have suggested earlier, as an aesthetics darkened in Baudelaire's terms by the grim shadow of original sin.

In *Les Fleurs du Mal* sin itself is Baudelaire's most terrible subject, for his Catholic background had left in his thought a peculiarly acute and hopeless sense of the evil in man. Thus his ideas of love and woman were inseparably related to the idea of sin; and the unnatural violence of his thought in this regard is all too clear when, in the *Intimate Journals,* he remarks that "woman is natural, that is to say abominable," refers to "the natural ferocity of love," likens the act of love itself to a torture or a surgical operation, notes that in love the one who loves the less of two lovers or who is the more self-possessed will be the executioner or the surgeon and the other the victim, and observes finally that "the unique and supreme voluptuous pleasure of love lies in the certainty of doing evil."

One is hardly surprised, then, to find love treated most often by Baudelaire from the viewpoint of despair. He seems driven by an agonizing nostalgia of the flesh, but has no hope for consolation

or enduring satisfaction. And so it is that he writes in the cycle of
poems to his mulatto mistress, Jeanne Duval:

> ... tu me parais, ornement de mes nuits,
> Plus ironiquement accumuler les lieues
> Qui séparent mes bras des immensités bleues.

> [... you seem to me, ornament of my nights,
> More ironically to increase the leagues
> That separate my arms from the blue immensities.]

The harshest epithets in the love poems to his various mistresses
show Baudelaire's recurrent misery in sensuality: "impure woman"
... "drinker of the world's blood" ... "blind, deaf machine, rich
in cruelties" ... "queen of sins" ... "vile animal" ... "vessel of
sorrow" ... "implacable and cruel beast" ... "pitiless demon."

Yet Baudelaire wrote in a famous letter that "woman is the
being who projects the greatest shadow or the greatest light into
our dreams. Woman is fatally suggestive; she lives with another
life than her own; she lives spiritually in the imaginations that she
haunts and enriches." Some of his poems to Marie Daubrun and
to Mme Sabatier are Platonic idealizations of woman; and, for
Jeanne Duval (along with such bitter and cruel erotic poems as
"Sed non satiata," "The Vampire," and "Duellum"), we find the
voluptuous and tender verses of "The Balcony." For all the agony
that they experienced together, Jeanne Duval was undoubtedly the
person, along with his mother, whom Baudelaire loved most in his
life. And so he can write, in the four poems called "Un fantôme"
("A Ghost"), long after Jeanne has lost her health and her youth
and her beauty, that in the shadows of his unfathomable sorrow a
spectral figure takes shape — graceful and shining. When it attains
its full form he recognizes Jeanne: "It is She! dark and yet lumi-
nous." The perfume of her pure youth seems a magic charm like
the scent of incense in a church, and he recalls how jewels and
furniture and the materials of her dress all served to set off her
voluptuous beauty. Then he remembers her as she is now in reality,
ravaged by disease:

> La Maladie et la Mort font des cendres
> De tout le feu qui pour nous flamboya.
> De ces grands yeux si fervents et si tendres,

De cette bouche où mon cœur se noya,
... ...
Que reste-t-il? ...
... ...

Noir assassin de la Vie et de l'Art,
Tu ne tueras jamais dans ma mémoire
Celle qui fut mon plaisir et ma gloire!

[Illness and Death turn to ashes
All the fire that blazed for us.
What is left now of those great eyes
    so glowing and tender,
And of that mouth where my heart was drowned....
... ...
[O Time!] dark murderer of Life and of Art,
You will never kill in my memory
The woman who was once my pleasure and my glory!]

Baudelaire sees voluptuous enjoyment on the whole as leading to remorse, and he refers to "the whip of Pleasure, that merciless executioner." In a powerful poem called "Femmes damnées" ("Damned Women"), one of the six poems condemned by the court, he describes the hellish descent of two Lesbians into a Dantesque Inferno. The rhythms of the original verses are an important part of the hypnotic horror of the poem:

    —Descendez, descendez, lamentables victimes,
    Descendez le chemin de l'enfer éternel!
    Plongez au plus profond du gouffre, où tous les crimes,
    Flagellés par un vent qui ne vient pas du ciel,
    Bouillonnent pêle-mêle avec un bruit d'orage.

    [—Descend, descend, lamentable victims,
    Descend the road of eternal Hell!
    Plunge to the depths of the gulf where all crimes,
    Whipped by a wind that is not from the sky,
    Come billowing pell-mell with the sound of a storm.]

These are clearly Dante's storm-winds blowing the carnal sinners as they were blown in life by the dark winds of their passions. And so it is, ultimately, always with the sensual pleasures in the thought of Baudelaire.

We have seen earlier, in the verses "To the Reader," the terrible role of Ennui or Spleen in Baudelaire's poems. The "delicate monster's" presence is usually attended by despairful imagery: deserts, frozen suns, green waters of Lethe, spiders and their webs, long funeral processions, lowering skies, sheets of rain that resemble prison bars, the tolling of a cracked bell, the dull sound of falling logs as firewood is unloaded in courtyards at the end of autumn.

One of Baudelaire's most remarkable symbols of boredom — as memorable in its way as Eliot's coffee-spoons — is an old deck of playing-cards, whose Jack of Hearts and Queen of Spades "talk in sinister fashion of their dead loves." But above all in Baudelaire's depiction of boredom there is the image of the slow, inexorable passing of time, which envelops the poet like an immense snowfall or ticks away in a clock's remorseless warnings 3600 times an hour. The supreme horror, amidst the boredom, is that, while to man the taedium of life seems endless, when his time on this earth finally runs out it is too late for repentance. And so the poet writes in his terror at the passing hours:

> The day declines; night comes on; *remember!*
> The abyss is always thirsty; the water-clock runs dry.

Man's dignity for Baudelaire was related to the boundless nature of his longing. In contrast with his friend Gautier who called himself primarily "a man for whom the visible world exists," Baudelaire wrote that through every window he saw only the infinite, and it was this unappeased longing that made him love the sea and that made the idea of the voyage so vital a part of his imagination. He discovered in what he called "the immense, tumultuous, green sea" an image of man and "the humors, the agonies and the ecstasies of all souls who have lived, are living, and will live hereafter!" Yet the sea is not so vast as human longing, and in "The Voyage," his major poem on death, Baudelaire describes how we set out on the rhythm of the wave,

> Berçant notre infini sur le fini des mers. . . .

"cradling the infinite within us on the finite of the seas." The poem is the last of *Les Fleurs du Mal* and brings to a rather ambiguous conclusion the volume's numerous and varied references

to death. The final verses have a strange power, but they leave us
still in doubt as to what Baudelaire's ultimate word might be:

> O Mort, vieux capitaine, il est temps! levons l'ancre!
> Ce pays nous ennuie, ô Mort! Appareillons!
> Si le ciel et la mer sont noirs comme de l'encre,
> Nos cœurs que tu connais sont remplis de rayons!
>
> Verse-nous ton poison pour qu'il nous réconforte!
> Nous voulons, tant ce feu nous brûle le cerveau,
> Plonger au fond du gouffre, Enfer ou Ciel, qu'importe?
> Au fond de l'Inconnu pour trouver du *nouveau!*
>
> [O Death, old Captain, it is time! let us weigh anchor!
> This world bores us, O Death! Let us get under way!
> If sky and sea are black as ink,
> Our hearts that you know are filled with rays of light!
>
> Pour out your poison to comfort us!
> We desire, so fiercely this fire burns our brain,
> To plunge to the depths of the abyss, what matter
>   whether it be Heaven or Hell?
> To the depths of the Unknown to find something *new!*]

* * *

Now, by way of ending, we come to the part of *Les Fleurs du
Mal* called "Tableaux Parisiens" ("Parisian Scenes"), that marvellous division of the poems in which Baudelaire transmits to us
over the years his imaginative evocation of the teeming life of the
great French capital in the mid-nineteenth century. Paris has
changed since then, just as the poet himself wrote of its changing
a hundred years ago:

> —Le vieux Paris n'est plus (la forme d'une ville
> Change plus vite, hélas! que le cœur d'un mortel)....
>
> [Old Paris is no more (the form of a city
> Changes more swiftly, alas! than a mortal heart)....]

But one has only to recall the first verses of "Les Petites Vieilles"
("The Little Old Women") in the "Tableaux Parisiens" to have the
wonder and mystery of Baudelaire's Paris rise up before his eyes:

> Dans les plis sinueux des vieilles capitales,
> Où tout, même l'horreur, tourne aux enchantements....

[In the sinuous folds of old capitals,
Where everything, even horror, turns to enchantments. . . .]

As I read these lines I see again the Paris of the Latin Quarter as I knew it thirty years ago.

And so it is that Baudelaire's evocation of the Paris of his day in *Les Fleurs du Mal* survives for us with a strangeness and mystery and beauty unique in literature. Only Villon and Balzac are comparable with him here, and in neither of these great writers is there so brooding and concentrated a spiritual quality as in Baudelaire. The moral and spiritual malaise of an age is in these pages; and it is an uneasiness of the spirit that remains with us, intensified and unrelieved, in our time.

In his *Salon of 1846,* Baudelaire comments on what he calls "a new and special beauty, which is not that of either Achilles or Agamemnon." He found this in Paris, and he wrote of it: "Parisian life is rich in poetic and marvellous subjects. The marvellous envelops us and permeates us like the atmosphere; but we do not see it." Baudelaire identifies here "a new element," which he calls *la beauté moderne* (modern beauty); and in Balzac and his heroes he finds something (greater than in the heroes of the *Iliad*) which he designates under the complex and rather ironic term, "l'héroïsme de la vie moderne" ("the heroism of modern life") — a phrase peculiarly pertinent, in Baudelaire's terms, for our own uneasy age.

In the first of the "Tableaux Parisiens" ("Paysages" ["Landscapes"]), Baudelaire says that he intends to compose his "eclogues" in a garret high above Paris, where he can see the tall church steeples "and the vast skies that make one dream of eternity." Here he can watch the seasonal changes in the great city and see the Parisian mists and the evening star rising and lamps at windows and "the moon pouring out its pale enchantment." In the following poems we have what may be said to constitute a day and a night of Parisian life, a period from sunrise to dawn of the following day (roughly the time-limit of ancient tragedy); and we shall trace briefly here some of its details from the verses of Baudelaire.

In "Le Soleil" the sun enters, like a kindly father, a poet and a king, to reanimate nature and bring joy and nobility to mankind. Then a red-haired beggar-girl appears ("A une mendiante rousse"), so beautiful, in spite of her rags, that she would have stirred desires in the Valois kings and inspired sonnets in Remy Belleau. But she goes along the street begging, and the poet cannot even afford the cheap trinkets that attract her glance as she passes by.

Baudelaire crosses the street near the Louvre and notices how the Paris he knows is changing ("Le Cygne"). Suddenly he thinks of Andromache and of a great white swan he once saw that had escaped from its cage and was dragging its magnificent plumage along the dusty Parisian street. The two beautiful figures, the swan and the lonely, captive widow of Hector — both separated forever from what they love — combine in the poet's mind to form an allegory of exile. He thinks of other lonely figures in the great capital — of a consumptive Negress, walking through the mud and seeking beyond the immense wall of Parisian mist "the absent coconut palms of proud Africa" — of orphaned children who are withering away like flowers — of whoever has lost what can never be found again. And the poem closes on this note of loneliness:

Thus in the forest where my mind is exiled
An old Memory sounds a full blast on the horn!
I think of the sailors forgotten on an island,
Of the captives and the conquered! . . . Of many others, besides!

Then, from the mysterious channels of the great city, out of the filthy, yellow mist, a hideous old man appears, bent over at right angles and leaning on a cane ("Les Sept Vieillards"). He has a beard stiff as a sword-blade, and his eyes are as malignant as if they had been steeped in gall. He is followed by another figure just like him . . . and another . . . and another, until seven sinister old men, all in the same hideous image, walk by with the same step towards an unknown destination. The hallucinative vision leaves the poet close to madness, and he flees to his room and locks himself in, terrified at the possibility of seeing an eighth old man emerge from the Parisian mists.

Sometimes, though, Baudelaire watches the old women of the city ("Les Petites Vieilles") with a sympathy that recalls Villon's for La Belle Heaulmière in the shadows of mediaeval Paris so long before. These were the young Parisian women of yesterday. They move now like marionettes, their bodies broken, misshapen, and shrunken by the years. Baudelaire writes, "Let us love them. They are still souls." Their eyes are young like those of little girls full of wonder at everything that shines; but yet they are "wells made of a million tears." These are the beautiful actresses, the faithful and faithless wives, the martyred mothers of other days. Children and drunk men make fun of them, and no one greets them kindly as they suffer in their strange destinies. They are human wreckage, "ripe for eternity." The poet follows them very tenderly in his thought, for they seem to be his family; and he bids them each evening a solemn farewell, thinking it may indeed be the last. And so he wonders in the final verses of the poem:

> Where will you be tomorrow, octogenarian Eves,
> Upon whom weighs the awful claw of God?

Next some of the blind people of Paris pass by ("Les Aveugles") with their faces turned forever upward toward the heavens — "terrible, strange, like sleepwalkers" as they go through their "unbounded darkness, that brother of eternal silence." But, for all their suffering, Baudelaire finds himself even more lost than they; and, amidst the wild uproar of Paris trying to amuse itself, he wonders what it is that all those blind people seek in the sky.

Suddenly, a beautiful woman appears in the crowd ("A une Passante") and disappears like a lightning-flash, leaving behind awakened and unfulfilled longings. Then, in the bookstalls along the quays, the poet discovers an anatomy chart with skeletons digging in the earth ("Le Squelette Laboureux"), and he wonders grimly whether there is, after all, any rest for mankind even in death.

At last twilight comes over Paris ("Le Crépuscule du Soir"), bringing solace to suffering and rest to the weary scholars and working men. But it is the hour also that awakens unhealthy demons in the great city. Prostitution lights up in the streets and is busy in its mysterious ways. Kitchens hiss with evening meals, and one hears the sounds of the theatres and orchestras. Gambling halls are filled with swindlers and courtesans, and merciless thieves set about breaking into houses and strong-boxes to gain their livelihood and buy their women clothes. But the poet summons his soul to turn inward upon itself in this darkening hour. Night is coming on, and in the hospitals some will never again be home with those they love; but most of them have never had a home and never really been alive.

The scene shifts to a gambling hall ("Le Jeu") where dishonored men and women watch feverishly the fate of their games; and, in spite of their degradation, the poet envies them their preference for suffering to death and hell to nothingness.

Then comes a "Danse Macabre" drawn from a figurine by the sculptor Ernest Christophe. Here a coquettish female skeleton, whose deep eyes are "made of emptiness and shadows," weaves flowers about her skull as she prepares for "the universal swing of the dance of death."

An indolent beauty passes by ("L'Amour du Mensonge"), and her ripe loveliness reminds the poet that melancholy eyes often conceal a nullity deeper and more empty than the heavens. But he worships her beauty, however stupid or indifferent she may be.

He recalls (XIV) the small white house where he lived as a child and the late sunlight falling over the long, silent dinners there; and he remembers a serving-woman who loved him long ago in his childhood (XV). She is dead now, and he thinks how lonely the dead must be when October winds blow over the Parisian cemeteries and when the winter snows begin to melt away. He wonders what he could say to the dead woman if some cold, blue December night he should find her in a chair by the fire with tears falling from her empty eyes.

When the mists and rains of late autumn come ("Brumes et Pluies") and one hears the rusty weathercocks turning in the long nights, Baudelaire imagines the pleasures of love lulling his grief in the moonless dark. Then he has a strange vision ("Rêve Parisien") that seems to come from an opium dream. The whole countryside is without vegetation, and one sees monotonously only metal, marble and water. There are stairways and arcades, pools and waterfalls. Space is limitless, and one comes upon unheard-of precious stones and magic flowers, vast rivers, and gulfs of diamonds. All things seem crystal-clear, and over the whole vision there hovers "(Everything for the eye, nothing for the ears) A silence of eternity." But when he awakens it is the horrible present in his wretched room, and his clock is striking the hour.

The last poem of the series is called "Le Crépuscule du Matin" ("Morning Twilight"). Reveille sounds in the barracks, and the morning wind blows on the lanterns. This is the hour when the brown adolescents toss on their pillows because of their dreams. The first lamps are lighted. The air is full of the sound of things fleeing away, "and man is weary of writing and woman of love." Smoke comes from chimneys, and the women of pleasure sleep stupidly with open mouths. The poor stir up their fires and blow on their cold fingers, and women in childbirth have the added sufferings of cold and nagging want. A cock-crow in the distance sounds like a sob cut off by blood. Mist rises like a sea around the buildings. People are dying in the hospitals. The roués return home, broken by their search for pleasure; and, as the rose and green dawn comes shivering up the deserted Seine, sombre Paris rubs its eyes and, like a hard-working old man, picks up its tools for the new day's toil.

* * *

In *Les Fleurs du Mal* Baudelaire affords us an unforgettable representation of the beauty and sadness and confusion and suffering of what he called "the heroism of modern life." His dark view of man and the human situation and his own spiritual, moral and physical anguish clearly lie behind the poems, whose strange and at times perverse beauty we have considered in some detail this evening. Yet beyond the sufferings and despair and boredom in *Les Fleurs du Mal* we find still an ardent spirituality and a consciousness, however dim and wavering, of eternal values. If we see the poems as Flowers of Evil and Flowers of Suffering we must recall that Baudelaire still recognized in man's nature the mark of the infinite and that he did not see human suffering merely in terms of sterile misery.

Evelyn Underhill, in her beautiful book on *Mysticism,* refers to suffering as "the 'gymnastic of Eternity,' the 'terrible initiative caress of God,'" and notes that "the highest types have accepted it eagerly and willingly, have found in Pain the grave but kindly teacher of immortal secrets, the conferer of liberty, even the initiator into amazing joys." Baudelaire did not attain completely to such mystical understanding; but he realized, as a great poet must, the relationship between suffering and the creation of beauty, and he wrote of it that "it is one of the prodigious privileges of

Art that ... *suffering* [*la douleur*] put to rhythm and cadence may fill the mind with a calm *joy*." It is significant here that Baudelaire underlines both *joy* and *suffering* as if to further emphasize their inter-relationship.

For Baudelaire there was a dignity and even a purifying grace in human suffering, and he depicts it on occasion, as we have seen, with a profound understanding and sympathy that seem to me unique in the literature of his age and perhaps, apart from Villon, unique in the whole of French letters. He proclaims suffering the only nobility that earth and hell cannot erode; and he writes of it in the poem called "Benediction":

> —Soyez béni, mon Dieu, qui donnez la souffrance
> Comme un divin remède à nos impuretés
> Et comme la meilleure et la plus pure essence
> Qui prépare les forts aux saintes voluptés!
>
> [Praised may you be, my God, who give suffering
> As a divine remedy for our impurities
> And as the best and purest essence
> That prepares those who are strong for holy joys!]

In incomplete verses intended as an epilogue for the second edition of his poems Baudelaire tells of his love for the city of Paris and of its "taste for the infinite"; and he calls upon its angels, dressed in purple, hyacinth and gold, to

> ... be witnesses that I have done my duty
> like a perfect chemist and like a holy soul.

Then he turns to the city itself for the last two lines:

> Car j'ai de chaque chose extrait la quintessence,
> Tu m'as donné ta boue et j'en ai fait de l'or.
>
> [For I have from each thing extracted its quintessence,
> You gave me your mire and I changed it to gold.]

II

ECHOES IN THE DARK CORRIDOR:
FLAUBERT'S VISION OF LIFE AND DEATH IN
MADAME BOVARY

> "The future was a corridor completely dark with its door shut fast at the end."
>
> *Madame Bovary*

IN THE FIRST LECTURE of the present series, we examined the powerful alchemy in the poems of Baudelaire and saw the darkness of a world where hope of salvation was dim at best, but where a great poet still kept a brooding sense of individual man's spiritual survival — his abiding relation with the infinite. This evening I shall bring before you an even more sombre vision of the lot of man — the terrible vision of Gustave Flaubert as I find it in one of the greatest of all French novels, *Madame Bovary*.

It is ironic that, for his masterpiece, Flaubert should have been subject to trial in a French law court, the same year as Baudelaire for *Les Fleurs du Mal* (1857) and, as we saw in a previous lecture, with the same charges of offenses against religion and *bonnes mœurs*. Unlike Baudelaire a little later in the year, Flaubert was acquitted of all charges. Today *Madame Bovary* is considered one of the world's great novels — and critics are still at work discovering what it has to say to us. Allen Tate has written that with Flaubert the novel has at last caught up with poetry, and I believe a careful reading of the book will make evident what he means. For *Madame Bovary* is a poem — and it is one of the saddest and most arresting poems in modern letters.

I think often of the day, many years ago, when my wife and I were discussing *The Scarlet Letter,* which she was then teaching in a course in the University at Chapel Hill, and of how I was enthralled at her account of what she was doing in class with Hawthorne's great novel. Strange forces emerged in a way I had not been aware of before in my reading, and the novel itself took on a new and more mysterious kind of life. Later, in rereading *Madame Bovary,* I began to sense an undercurrent there, too, of something I had missed before; and I set about trying to discover what I could find of its nature and significance in the novel. Students and other friends outside the classroom had suggestions when I discussed what I was doing, and in 1949 I published an article in *Studies in Philology* on "Flaubert's Correspondence and the Ironic and Symbolic Structure of *Madame Bovary.*" Since then, over the years, in many rereadings and through accumulating scholarship, seminars, class discussions, and numerous student insights I have come to sense and to identify further details of what apparently lay behind those first impressions. In my lecture before you this evening I shall try, then, to bring some of these and my earlier suggestions together as clearly as I can in an attempt to show how they relate to the sombre vision of life and death that is mirrored in Flaubert's masterpiece.

First of all, it is important to realize something of the sensitive and rich mind and spirit behind the novel; and for immediate and direct touch on these we have Flaubert's remarkable corresponden-ce, much of it written while he was composing *Madame Bovary.* Here we see something of the author's thoughts and his favorite readings and can obtain glimpses of some of his deepest emotions and inner commitments. I know few letters comparable to the best of these for a revelation of the joys and sufferings of the creative mind. In a passage here, Flaubert writes: "At heart I am a mystic, and I believe in nothing." For a religious mind, this would be a strange sort of mysticism; but the evidence of what it meant to Flaubert as an artist is perhaps best clarified in the following quotation from one of his letters to his mistress, Louise Colet. Here we can obtain a glimpse, if only for a moment, of Flaubert's sense of the artist's austere loneliness and exaltation; and the words provide an almost visionary insight into the kind of sacrifice and inspiration that lay behind Flaubert's own achievement:

> ... Is it not with the artist's life, or rather with a work of art to be accomplished as with a great mountain to be climbed? A hard journey and one that demands an unrelenting will! At first you perceive from below a lofty peak; in the skies it is sparkling with purity, terrifying in height! and yet it calls to you for that very reason. You set out, but at each plateau of the way, the summit grows larger, the horizon recedes, you go through precipices, fears of falling and discouragements, it is cold! and the eternal whirlwind of the lofty regions tears from you in passing the very last shred of your clothing; the earth is lost forever and the goal doubtless will not be attained. It is the hour when you consider your weariness, when you look with sudden terror upon the cracks in your skin. You have nothing but an irresistible desire to mount higher, to finish with it all, to die. And yet, sometimes, a gust of winds from the heavens comes and unveils before your dazzled eyes innumerable, infinite, marvelous perfections! You see men twenty thousand feet beneath you, an Olympian wind fills your giant lungs and you see yourself as a colossus with the whole world for your pedestal. Then the mist falls again and you go on blindly! — blindly tearing your nails on the rocks and weeping because of the loneliness. No matter! let us die in the snow, in the white grief of our desiring, to the murmur of the torrents of the Mind and our face turned toward the sun.

It seems to me especially significant that Flaubert wrote thus of "a work of art to be accomplished" at the very time he was composing the novel with which we are concerned this evening.

* * *

In considering *Madame Bovary* it should be useful to recall very briefly the general line of action in the story; for, as Aristotle once wrote, you can have a tragedy without character, but you cannot have one without plot. Plot (what happens in the narrative) is naturally very important in a novel like *Madame Bovary,* though it is in fact only the central nervous system, as it were, for many other elements in the work.

The structure of the action here is tripartite; and a notable aspect of the novel is the recurrence of elements in threes — not only in the episodes, but in central male characters, in symbols, and in narrative details. Thus Emma's mature experience falls into three parts, each of which finds her primarily concerned with one of the three men in her adult life. And we cannot fail to relate this to the three layers of her wedding cake, so variously described — and to the three so various Cupids placed separately in the three separate parts of the novel — and to the three separate coffins, each of a different material, in which Emma is finally buried. Nor can we fail to remark the pertinence here of the three major symbols in the book — the Spider, the Man with the Lathe, and the Blind Man — which are introduced, in turn, in the first, second, and third parts of the narrative and come together all three, as we shall see, in terrible union with other symbols, only at Emma's death. All this suggests in advance something of the structure of *Madame Bovary* as a work of art; but we need to recall the basic details of plot in order to proceed.

Briefly, *Madame Bovary* is the story of Emma Rouault, a young farm girl brought up in an Ursuline convent where she acquires a headful of sentimental values from keepsake books and romantic novels and poems. She marries a widower, Charles Bovary, a plodding, kindly-intentioned, but remarkably insentient provincial health officer, and suffers from the terrible boredom of her life. At a nobleman's château she attends a ball that introduces her to a world of luxury for which she thinks herself intended; and she never recovers from its influence. The Bovarys move from Tostes to another town, Yonville l'Abbaye, where Emma has a daughter when she had hoped for a son; and then the old boredom and monotony weigh down on her again. Emma is seduced and takes a lover (Rodolphe Boulanger), who abandons her — and then another lover (Léon Dupuis); and she ruins herself and her husband with her extravagance. Then, disillusioned in her second love affair, overwhelmed by debts, and seeing no way out, she commits suicide by taking arsenic. Soon Charles Bovary himself dies after finally discovering his wife's infidelities. Their daughter is sent to work in a spinning mill, and in the last sentence of the book M. Homais, the druggist, who stands for compromise, dishonesty, and shrewd, insistent self-promotion, has just been awarded the Cross of the Legion of Honor.

The plot line sounds banal; but Flaubert has arranged so terrible a framework for the fate of Emma Bovary and used so effectively his half-hidden patterns of symbol and suggestion that the reader is likely to feel himself, as Flaubert hoped he would, "crushed without knowing why." In the remaining pages of my paper this evening I shall try to show something of this and the grim vision it affords us of Flaubert's view of life and death — his conception of the fate of man.

I

As one reads *Madame Bovary* one finds recurrent images and symbols that are seen finally to be moving at the very core of Emma's fate. Colors, especially blue and green, appear to assume symbolic reference; and it seems pertinent to remark that we see Emma first in a blue merino dress, and that she reaches into a blue bowl for the arsenic with which she commits suicide, and that when her father comes to her funeral he has put on a new shirt whose blue coloring comes off from his tears and leaves blue marks on his face.

Green and velvet, on the other hand, seem to be associated with what Emma wants and can never quite obtain. Thus, the cigar-case from La Vaubyessard is of green silk — when Emma first sees Rodolphe he is wearing a green velvet coat — Rodolphe dresses in velvet and Léon in green when each first seduces Emma — the merchant Lheureux displays his wares from a green packing case — and Charles, ironically, after Emma's death, provides that "a great piece of green velvet" be placed over her caskets where she lies in her white wedding dress. We may recall here that the base of Emma's wedding cake was blue and that its top layer represented a green meadow. Though a single color does not always function in the same way, colors thus have on occasion an echoing quality that refers back and forward through the narrative as one reads. And ultimately, as with the great piece of green velvet, such echoes seem to be part of a terrible irony.

The names of Flaubert's characters provide some of the richest and most varied ironic patterns in *Madame Bovary;* and sometimes to perceive their richness one must recall that Flaubert read his lines aloud to himself in his famous *gueuloir,* so that sounds often rise imperiously above the visual spellings in the names to provide echoes for the listener that the purely visual reader might not be conscious of at all.

One can hardly conceive here a given name less likely than Emma's to please Flaubert's romantic heroine; and Emma will have none of it when Charles suggests it as the name for their newly born daughter. Among the women Emma admired Flaubert cites such figures as Héloïse and Virginie (of *Paul et Virginie*), and he tells us that she liked the name Léocadie. It can hardly be by chance that Flaubert gives the first of these names (Héloïse) to Charles Bovary's first wife, and the second (Virginie) with added semantic irony to Rodolphe's mistress, and the third (Léocadie) to the woman whom Léon marries after Emma's death. At first glance, this treatment of names may seem merely whimsical; but a further examination of Flaubert's practice shows how deliberate it is and suggests that Flaubert meant to create a pattern of fatality in the very names of his characters. I believe we can show that this fatality is one from which Emma had no means of escape. Thus the names of Flaubert's characters here are as inevitable a part of Emma's destiny as are in general the recurrent echoes from the past in her future, which she once saw prophetically in words we have used for an epigraph as "a corridor completely dark with its door shut fast at the end."

Emma's last name (*Rou*ault), like the town of *Rou*en, has the wheel in it *(la roue),* a recurrent image in the novel; and it is of interest here that Flaubert referred to his own life as a wheel *(un rouage)* while he was working on *Madame Bovary.* If one listens, one can hear the wheel again in the name of Catherine Le*roux,* the old woman at the Agricultural Meeting who had been reduced to almost animal placidity by fifty-four years of agricultural servitude and who is given in recognition of all this a medal worth 25 francs before a platform full of bourgeois functionaries. One may recall here the fine irony in the fact that St. Catherine herself was bound to the martyr's wheel.

The names of Emma's husband and lovers all have likewise the mark of this structural irony. Charles Bovary is thus a name subtly woven into the elements of Emma's fate. Charles means "manly," which is remote at least from Emma's estimate of her husband. The name Bovary, moreover, is chosen with meticulous care. It is clearly related to something bovine or oxlike, and among the Latins we find in fact the adjective *bovarius* in the phrase *forum bovarium* for the market where horned cattle were sold. We may recall here the description of Charles going along on horseback in the early morning thinking of the pleasures of the night with Emma — as Flaubert puts it, "ruminant son bonheur," which means "thinking of his happiness" and also *"chewing the cud of his happiness,"* like a ruminant. The pertinence for a Bovary is clear enough.

Rodolphe Boulanger de la Huchette, the first of Emma's lovers, has quite appropriately the wolf in his given name. But his lively animality is diluted by the trade name Boulanger *(baker),* and la Huchette, the name of his estate, means something like "little bread-bin." We shall see later how all this is linked with a very sombre structure in Flaubert's novel.

Léon Dupuis, Emma's second lover, has a proud name from the king of beasts; but Léon, who takes his meals at the *Lion d'Or (The Golden Lion),* an establishment itself of little glory, is a cowardly creature, hardly deserving his lordly appellation.

When we move from these three individuals (all with names of beasts) back into the general nomenclature of Flaubert's characters it may come as a surprise to find the pattern of ironic meaning continued in the novel. The town of Yonville l'Abbaye, to which the Bovarys move from Tostes, is itself described as looking from a distance "lying out along the river shore like a cowherd taking a siesta at the water's edge"; and the mayor of the town is M. Tu*vache* (cow). All this suggests that the motif of oxlike or cowlike insensibility is persistent in the structure of *Madame Bovary*. But when Flaubert gives the name Léocadie Lebœuf (ox) to the woman from Bondeville whom Léon marries after Emma's death, he seems quite clearly to be telling us that just as Emma Rouault was caught by marrying a Bovary when she tried to escape her lot, so her lover at the last is caught in marrying someone named Lebœuf.

There are numerous further ironies in the names of Flaubert's characters. When Emma and Charles arrive at Yonville l'Abbaye from Tostes they are brought in a coach called "l'Hirondelle," the French name for the swallow, the harbinger of spring. It is in the "Hirondelle" that Emma will go so often to see her lover Léon in Rouen; and Emma's dreams are described on one occasion as falling like wounded swallows in the mire. The driver of the "Hirondelle" is named Hivert — and, though the name is spelled with a *t,* the word is clearly *hiver* (winter) for the ear. It is in the "Hirondelle" that Emma first feels the cold of death upon her as she comes back from Rouen.

But if there is an ominous irony in the relation between Hivert and the "Hirondelle," this is not apparent when the coach and its driver first appear bringing the Bovarys to Yonville l'Abbaye. In fact, it seems a very auspicious moment for them in their new home when Emma descends from the coach and is followed by Félicité and M. Lheureux, whose names mean in turn "happiness" and "the happy (*or* the fortunate) one." But, in reality, Félicité is a rather sad little maid, whose name so struck Flaubert that he gave it many years later to the lonely heroine of *Un cœur simple;* and M. Lheureux is the shrewd draper and financier who ruins Emma and Charles financially and is ultimately responsible for their downfall.

In service at the inn where the Bovarys take their first meal in Yonville l'Abbaye there are a club-footed stable-boy named Hippolyte and a maid-of-all-work named Artémise. Flaubert surely knew what he was doing in selecting these names, which can hardly have failed to recall to his savagely ironical mind the story of Hippolytus and his worship of the goddess Artemis. The names are not identical, for Artemis does not have the final *e* in French; but Artémis and Artémise are so close that in conjunction with Hippolyte the echoes seem all too clear. (The irony proliferates here if one thinks also of the purity of Hippolytus and of King Mausolus's widow Artémise, a famous symbol of conjugal fidelity.) Moreover, Hippolyte, the club-footed stable-boy is, in fact, as his Greek name implies, a "looser of horses"; and we learn that the special kind of club foot he has is called an *equinus* (thus underlining still further the idea of the horse in his name). It is Charles' bungling effort later to operate on Hippolyte's foot that puts the final barrier between the Bovarys; and Hippolyte's horrible cry at the amputation of his gangrenous leg with its seeping black liquid provides a grim part of Flaubert's ironic structure in the novel. The surgeon who performs the amputation and who admits that he would as soon carve a Christian as a fowl is ironically named Canivet (a diminutive of the French word for knife).

Flaubert himself wrote that the name of the druggist Homais came from *homo* (man); but it is a diminutive or perverted form and is clearly meant to reflect adversely on its owner's character. The name of the nurse, mère Rollet, suggests perhaps a wheel or its rolling motion. At all events, the nurse is spinning at a very crucial moment in Emma's life, as we shall see hereafter. Even the name of Mlle Lempereur (the woman at Rouen who submits after Emma's death a bill for piano lessons she never gave) may enter the pattern. But here the name would seem to be directed against Napoleon III. It would be strange indeed to use such a name in such circumstances without thought of the Emperor.

Sometimes there are persistent overtones in names that seem to fit into other patterns of meaning in the novel. For example, when Emma goes to the estate of the Marquis d'Andervilliers where she enjoys the rapture of the ball, she was surely not conscious of the bovine syllable in its name, La *Vau*byessard. And when she admired there a slavering old imbecilic duke she would hardly have perceived in his name the *green* of La*verd*ière. But Flaubert may have heard it, as he may have heard the calf in La Vaubyessard. At all events, these kinds of ironies are recurrent in the names of Flaubert's characters, and they suggest the inescapable fatality in Emma's world.

Let me cite two other examples which seem to me most pertinent to this fixed order of things in Flaubert's universe for Emma Bovary. When Emma is about to have a child she wants a boy. She imagines him strong and dark and thinks how much freer a man is than a woman. Her son will realize the freedom and the sort of dreams of far away places that she herself has never been able to enjoy. She decides to call him George. But, as one might expect in Emma's world, when the child is born it is a girl — and Emma faints in disappointment. When she has to select the infant's name, she thinks of romantic heroines, refuses Charles' suggestion of Emma, and finally decides on Berthe, merely because she had heard a young woman called by that name at the ball at La Vaubyessard. Now Berthe means "bright" — and that in itself is ironic enough for a little girl who is sent after her parents' and grandmother's deaths to work in a spinning mill. But there is more than this in the name. One can hardly fail, if he will listen, to hear in Berthe an echo of "Les *Bert*aux," the name of the Rouault farm. So Emma's dreams and imaginings are always ultimately in the dark corridor of her fate — and when one hears the echoes there he knows that she is lost. Longing for a freedom, such as she herself has never known, for her imagined son, she decides in her innocence to call him George (farmer); and trying to link the name of her daughter with what she considers the ideal realization of her life, she decides to call her Berthe — and the ironic echo in both cases is from the farm from which she herself had sought escape in the world of Bovarys. And all this is not chance or idle whim — it is the terrible, fatal pattern in which Flaubert has framed the struggle of his heroine. Probably nowhere else in literature have the names of characters been shaped to so integral and terrible a revelation of an artist's view of life.

II

Before we turn to some of the separate individual symbols and images that recur and echo, as it were, and finally move together at Emma's death, I should like to examine an especially complex organization of imagery and symbol in the novel concerned with the relationship between love or the act of love and food or the processes and rituals of eating. This is one of the most intricately developed and one of the most cruel and ironic of all the echoing motifs in *Madame Bovary*.

In his youth, Flaubert once wrote to Ernest Chevalier: "Oh, how right Molière is to compare woman to a dish of soup. . . . Many men want to devour it, they burn their throats with it, and others come after. . . ." The remark is brutal and cynical; but nearly twenty years later a comparable imagery is developed at great length in *Madame Bovary,* and I believe that under careful examination it will reveal a very different attitude on the part of Flaubert — a deep and abiding sympathy with his unhappy heroine. It will show also something of the remarkably complex way in which Flaubert relates details of elaborate imagery and symbol immediately to the line of action and the meaning of his narrative.

Flaubert's equations here are deeply rooted in human experience. It has been said that "love and hunger govern the world"; and the blending or confusion of these two powerful human motivations is clearly evident. At vulgar levels, the unpleasant and shocking nature of verbal reference suggests widespread psychological patterns and analogies linking ideas of food and hunger with ideas of love and love-longing. Wentworth and Flexner's *Dictionary of American Slang* (1960) thus notes frequent evidence of man's relating sex and food, and remarks upon the apparent relationship between the two subjects at subconscious levels of perception. Such terms as *sugar, sweetheart* and *honey* or *honeymoon* imply equations of the gentler sort; and we are all familiar with the generally harmless cliché "You look good enough (or sweet enough) to eat!" But when, for example, Arnolphe says to Agnès in Molière's *L'école des femmes* (Act V, Sc. iv)

"Sans cesse, nuit et jour, je te caresserai,
Je te bouchonnerai, baiserai, mangerai. . . ."

[Endlessly, night and day, I shall caress you,
Rub you fondly, kiss you, *eat* you. . . .]

with the crescendo of amatory violence the final verb becomes ominous.

In such reference, the erotic symbolism of cherries and apples is elegant and very old in poetry. Without citing the more brutal and painful equations that occur in obscene slang we may, nevertheless, note the progressive decline of respect evident in such terms for a woman as *tomato, quail, dish,* and *tart* (the last of which began as a term of endearment). It will be amply evident hereafter that all this has its sombre pertinence to Flaubert's dark irony in his treatment of love and longing in the world of Emma Bovary.

One can hardly be surprised that a novel with the subtitle *Mœurs de province* (provincial *mores*) should have frequent reference to eating and drinking and smoking, that the table, the kitchen and the dining-room should figure prominently in its pages, and that food should be mentioned under many different circumstances. It thus seems entirely natural for Flaubert to describe Charles Bovary in his youth as a commonplace boy "who played at play-time, worked in study-hours, listened in class, slept well in his dormitory and ate heartily in the dining-hall." In one sentence with five images Flaubert here vividly presents young Charles Bovary as the incarnation of unimaginative mediocrity. It is of special interest that the final image, chosen for cumulative emphasis in the series, is of the youthful Charles eating. It is no surprise later to find (again in a single sentence) Charles Bovary as a young man becoming enthusiastic over Béranger, learning to make punch, and finally to make love.

At the feast for Charles' and Emma's wedding, Flaubert describes the food and drink in some detail. The masterpiece, which we have cited earlier, is a cake in several layers with a little Cupid on top in a chocolate swing, whose two supporting posts terminate in natural rose-buds. Here the erotic symbols of Cupid and swing and rose-buds are combined with the food reference in chocolate, and the pertinence to Emma's bridal night seems clearly apparent.

A few pages later the parallel between eating and the act of love is repeated in more precise terms in a passage from which we have already quoted for a different reference. After a night with Emma, Charles rides off, the sun on his back, the morning air in his nostrils, "his heart full of the joys of the night, his mind at peace, his flesh content"; and he goes *"ruminant son bonheur* like those who still savour, after dinner, the taste of the truffles they are digesting." Later Flaubert remarks that Charles has come to take Emma for granted. He embraces her at fixed times. It is like any one of a number of habits ... "like a dessert anticipated in advance after the monotony of dinner."

With the passing of time Emma realizes more and more clearly how insentient Charles is to her longing, and it seems to her that if he had shown even once any understanding, "a sudden abundance would have been set free from her heart, as the fruit falls from an espalier, when one puts his hand to it." We shall see hereafter how Flaubert develops this pathetic image and brings it to a cruelly ironic maturity in later pages of the novel. For the moment, we may note merely that Emma's longing for love and understanding is likened to fruit ready to fall from an espalier at the touch of a questing hand.

At the beginning of Part Two there is a description of the town and the inhabitants of Yonville l'Abbaye on the confines of Normandy, Picardy and the Ile de France. It is to Yonville that the Bovarys are moving, and Flaubert tells us that the worst cheeses of the region are made there.

Near the town is the cemetery, where at the time of the cholera the inhabitants of Yonville had knocked down a section of the wall and bought three acres of adjacent land for burial plots. Even the new space is now largely filled with graves; and we are told that the gravedigger and church beadle, Lestiboudois, has planted potatoes in the as yet unused part of the cemetery. The little plot of land becomes smaller from year to year, and in times of epidemics the gravedigger cannot decide whether to rejoice at the deaths or to be afflicted at the spreading graves that cut down his garden space. When the *curé* once said to him, "You feed on the dead, Lestiboudois" he was taken aback for a time; but Flaubert tells us that at the story's end Lestiboudois still continues to cultivate his potatoes and that "he even insists with assurance that they grow naturally."

In Part Two we meet the first of Emma's seducers — Rodolphe Boulanger, de la Huchette, whose last name (Baker) along with that of his estate (Little Bread-bin) has its own ironic pertinence in Flaubert's symbolic pattern of food and love. After his first sight of Emma, Rodolphe thinks, "Poor little woman! She is gaping after love like a carp after water on a kitchen table." Here again, the ironic reference is cruelly apparent in the relationship between kitchen, food and love. Rodolphe thinks how easily he could have Madame Bovary. "With three words of *galanterie,* she would adore you, I'm sure of it!" He has no thought for Emma's happiness. He can win her easily — yes, but how get rid of her afterwards? He thinks of his mistress Virginie and is irritated at recollection of her fondness for shrimp. As a first step toward seducing Emma he decides to bring the Bovarys some game, some poultry — and at need even to have himself bled.

At the Agricultural Meeting, while Rodolphe sets about seducing Emma, M. Lieuvain (the speaker) sets about seducing his rustic audience. The effect, with its alternate snatches of words as the two orators go about their business, is at once bitterly ironic and cruelly funny. M. Lieuvain is full of expansive eulogy for the hen: "Who has not often reflected," he asks, "on all the benefits we draw from this modest creature, this ornament of our chicken-yards, that furnishes at the same time a soft pillow for our beds, its succulent flesh for our tables, and eggs?" —Beds, succulent flesh and eggs! And Emma, still (in Rodolphe's earlier words) "gaping after love like a carp . . . on a kitchen table"!

Some weeks later, immediately after Emma's surrender in the forest, Rodolphe has a cigar in his mouth, as a man might after a meal.

The symbol of the burden in Emma's heart like the yield from an espalier waiting for a hand to touch it develops slowly to a peculiarly sad and ironic resolution. We are prepared for various kinds of fruits, and there is an early reference to apricots on an espalier in the Bovarys' first garden at Tostes. But the night that Rodolphe comes knowingly for the last time to a rendezvous with Emma, the symbol is brought into brilliant play. The lovers fall under the spell of the night — its fragance of syringas (symbolic of memories) and the great moonlight flashing on the river. They recall the tenderness of former days and both are deeply moved. Off in the night they hear nocturnal animals stirring, and now and then "a ripe peach falling all alone from the espalier" — the symbol of the longing in Emma's heart.

When Rodolphe returns home he goes over the souvenirs of his conquests — a handkerchief, a miniature of Emma, her love letters, bouquets, a garter, a black mask, pins, and hair of various colors, some of which breaks off at the pull of the opening hinge; and all of these souvenirs of his dead loves are kept in an old cookie-box! Rodolphe Boulanger de la Huchette!

After Rodolphe has written his hypocritical letter of farewell to Emma he sends it to her in a basket of apricots; and the fruit falls out on the floor from Emma's hands. When Charles' voice stops her from possible suicide, Emma returns to the kitchen where the evening meal is ready. The maid picks up the scattered apricots, and Charles holds out the basket to Emma. "Just smell! What a fragrance!" And he waves the basket under her nose. Then he eats some of the apricots and spits the seeds into his hand. At this moment Rodolphe's blue tilbury drives by at full speed, departing on a distant journey. Emma cries out and faints, overturning the table and all the dishes and all the food. Later Charles tells Homais that Emma had fainted quite without warning while she was eating apricots; and Homais remarks that odors have remarkable effects on impressionable natures, just as, for example, "*napeta cataria,* vulgarly called catnip" has a singularly aphrodisiac effect on cats.

This involved and ironic development of the symbol of Emma's longing in terms of ripe fruit waiting on an espalier for a hand to touch it, metamorphosed here into apricots from Rodolphe that are eaten by Charles, and finally into a reference to an aphrodisiac for cats, is one of the most startling examples of the so-called "maturing image" or "maturing symbol" in Flaubert. Nor is this the end. Léon is later described at Paris thinking of Emma. He had not lost all hope — and in his memory of her there was still for him something "like an uncertain promise swaying in the future, like a golden fruit, suspended on some fantastic branch."

In the third part of the book, the sombre development and dénouement of Léon's and Emma's love affair follow their meeting again at Rouen. In one ironic scene, Léon tries desperately to get away from dinner with Homais to go to his rendezvous with Emma. But Homais wants to talk about love and discusses the various qualities of German, French and Italian women. "What about Negresses?" asked the clerk. "That is the taste of an artist," said Homais. "Garçon! two demi-tasses!"

When Emma tries to borrow money from Maître Guillaumin, the notary, he is dining on a cutlet and drinking tea and wearing slippers that were a love gift. He stops eating and tries to embrace Emma, and she flees. Thereafter, failing to obtain help from Binet and finally from Rodolphe, she enters Homais' pharmacy, where she hears the sound of his family's forks striking against their plates in the dining-room. She gets the key to the Capharnaum from Justin, Homais' apprentice, on the pretense that she wants something to kill the rats that keep her from sleeping. Then she unlocks the door, takes the cork from the blue glass jar of arsenic, seizes a handful of the white powder, and literally eats it.

At Emma's burial we hear nothing of her lovers; but thereafter we are told that at midnight of her first night in the earth Rodolphe and Léon are asleep. Charles is talking late with his mother. But on Emma's grave a young boy is weeping. This is Justin, Homais' apprentice, who loved Emma with an adolescent love. Flaubert is unsparing here, as elsewhere in the novel, in his depiction of the lack of understanding among his characters. Just as there was no sympathetic comprehension of Emma's longing, so there is ironic misinterpretation of the grief of a young boy in the night:

> On the grave, between the fir trees, a child knelt weeping, and his breast, shaken by sobs, was racked in the darkness, under the compulsion of an immense regret, sweeter than the moon and deeper than night. Suddenly the gate creaked. It was Lestiboudois [the gravedigger], coming to look for his spade which he had forgotten a short while before. He recognized Justin climbing over the wall, and then he knew who was to be blamed for stealing his potatoes.

This last reference brings into focus various elements of Flaubert's ironic imagery. In the end, Emma becomes not truffles or a dessert after the monotony of dinner, as she had been for Charles; or a golden fruit on a branch, as she had been for Léon; or another conquest to be entered among the faded trophies in Rodolphe Baker's cookie-box — but a symbolic fertilizer for potatoes in the cemetery garden of the gravedigger, Lestiboudois, who feeds upon the dead.

III

As a prelude to our consideration of the three major symbols in *Madame Bovary,* I should like to examine very briefly a few of the numerous recurring thematic images that can be shown to relate most immediately at the last to Flaubert's symbolic structure in the novel: echoing voices, dust, and the wind.

Echoing voices provide some of the most eerily symbolic effects in all of Flaubert's maturing imagery; and these effects recall two memorable passages from Vergil and Ovid that may help us to see what Flaubert is doing here in *Madame Bovary*. The first of these occurs in the Fourth Book of the *Aeneid* (verses 165-168), where Vergil describes as follows the moment of Dido's surrender to Aeneas during the hunt when a storm drives the two leaders to shelter:

> To the same cave came Dido and the Trojan chief,
> Primal Earth and nuptial Juno gave the sign; fires flashed

from Heaven, the witness of their bridal and on the moun-
tain-top screamed the Nymphs. *

So much for the moment of love. But the very next verses are
chilling, indeed:

> That day was the first day of death, that first the cause
> of woe.

Ovid has Dido retell the episode in two ominous verses of the
Heroïdes (VII. 95-96), where she says of the cries she heard:

> I had heard a voice. I thought it was the marriage chant
> of the nymphs: it was really the Furies who gave the signal
> for my doom.

The numerous voices in *Madame Bovary* have a terrible part
among the echoes in Emma's dark corridor; and there are three
passages that seem to me especially pertinent here. When Rodolphe
is arranging the background for Emma's seduction at the Agricultural Meeting, their conversation turns to the subject of human
happiness. Emma asks whether one ever finds it, and Rodolphe
replies: "Yes, it comes one day." He is interrupted temporarily
by the orator Lieuvain, who is speaking, at the moment, of progress,
morality, and atmospheric disturbances. Then Rodolphe continues
on the subject of happiness:

> "It comes one day... one day, suddenly, and when
> you were despairing of it. Then horizons open, and it is like
> a voice crying: 'There it is!'...."

Twenty-five pages later, just after her surrender to Rodolphe in
the forest, Emma seems to realize this beguiling promise and to
hear at last the voice of happiness:

> The evening shadows were falling; sunlight from the
> horizon, passing between the branches, dazzled her eyes.
> Here and there, all about her, in the leaves and on the
> ground, spots of light were trembling, as if hummingbirds,

---

* Loeb revised edition (1947). The succeeding translation of Ovid is
from Arthur Palmer's edition of the *Heroïdes* (1898).

flying by, had scattered their feathers. There was no sound anywhere; something sweet seemed to be coming from the trees; she felt her heart, which was beginning to beat again, and the blood circulating in her flesh like a river of milk. Then, far away, beyond the woods, over the other hills, she heard a cry, vague and prolonged, a voice that trailed away [*se traînait*], and she listened to it silently, mingling like a music with the last vibrations of her shaken nerves. . . .

When Emma reaches home she is astonished at her face in the mirror. Her eyes are larger and darker and deeper than they have ever been. She feels transfigured, and repeats to herself: "I have a lover! a lover!"

But Emma has not really heard the voice of happiness; and nearly a hundred and fifty pages later in the book we hear prophetic echoes in the voice of the symbolic Blind Man, whose rôle we shall return to hereafter. The Blind Man is a terrifying sight. Covered with rags he wanders about the hillside, tapping with his stick. Liquids flow from the bleeding flesh of his eyelids and form green scabs all the way down to his nose with its black nostrils. When he throws back his head to speak, his bluish eyeballs roll horribly toward his temples. And he sings a little song as he follows the "Hirondelle." The words are innocent enough as Flaubert gives them here:

> "Often the warmth of a fair day
> Makes a young girl dream of love."

Flaubert says that in all the rest of the song there were birds and leaves and sunlight. We shall hear the rest of the song later, and it will not be quite so innocent at the last. But even here the voice of the Blind Man terrifies Emma, and we can see in the passage describing it that what Emma had thought earlier was the voice of happiness is echoing now with subtle changes:

> [The Blind Man's] voice, whining and weak at first, became shrill. It trailed away [*se traînait*] into the night, like the faint wailing of a vague distress; and through the chiming of the harness-bells, the murmur of the trees and the humming [*ronflement*] of the hollow box [the "Hirondelle"], it had about it something far-away that over-

whelmed Emma. It descended to the depths of her soul
like a whirlwind into an abyss and carried her away
through spaces of a boundless melancholy.

Certain words in the French here *(se traînait . . . le ronflement . . .
la boîte creuse . . . un tourbillon dans un abîme . . . la mélancolie)*
are all integral parts of Flaubert's narrative structure brought
together in this description of the Blind Man's song.

All through the novel there is recurrent dust, as if to keep us
mindful of the ruin of all things. Dust rises along the roads that
Emma goes, it pursues the rolling wheels of the "Hirondelle" (the
Swallow, the harbinger of spring), it covers Emma's wedding
bouquet, one smells it in Rodolphe's cookie-box amidst his
keepsakes and love letters, and we shall see it finally in a somewhat
different form combining with the major symbols at Emma's death.

And then there is the wind, which plays a continuing and
symbolic role in *Madame Bovary* and provides one of the strangest
echoing references in the novel. As in the *Inferno* of Dante's
Commedia, which Flaubert read while he was composing *Madame
Bovary,* the wind prefigures here the unruliness and violence of
human passions and their disruptive rôle in human lives. Whoever
has read the *Inferno* will recall the memorable passage on Paolo
and Francesca, in which Dante describes the carnal sinners forever
blown in the dark strife of winds like a flock of starlings in a winter
storm — and again like a flock of cranes crying as they make long
lines of themselves in the dark air. And so Emma is seen in
Madame Bovary, feeling herself "soft and completely abandoned
like the down of a bird turning in a tempest"; and when Léon
sends a boy to get the cab in which he intends to seduce Emma,
the lad runs down la Rue des Quatre Vents (the Street of the Four
Winds) in search of the vehicle. We shall see hereafter the terrible
recurrence — what we may call the echo at the last — of the wind
in the corridor and how it fits into the whole over-all structure of
the fate of Emma Bovary.

*   *   *

Now finally we arrive at the three major symbols — the Spider,
the Man with the Lathe, and the Blind Beggar; and we may remark
how carefully Flaubert introduces them, one after the other, into

the framework of his novel. First comes the Spider in Part One along with images of darkness and cold. Emma has been disillusioned in her life with Charles and wonders why she ever married. And Flaubert writes of her: ". . . Her life was cold as an attic with a window to the north, and the silent spider ennui was spinning its web in the shadow in every corner of her heart." We do not hear of the spider again for hundreds of pages; but it continues its dark work, and when it reappears Emma's life is almost done.

The second major symbol is the Man with the Lathe — Binet, the tax-collector, who is promptness personified, and who, we are told, has his own measuring-rod. Binet is presented as the epitome of bourgeois dullness — a man who spends his spare time in his attic turning out napkin-rings [!] on his lathe, whose humming sound [*ronflement*] can be heard as far as *The Golden Lion* all day long on Sunday and on clear afternoons. One of my friends has suggested that Binet's name may come from *bobiner* (to reel or wind on a bobbin); and this derivation would have a dreadful pertinence for what I see as Binet's symbolic role in *Madame Bovary*.

When Emma flees to the attic with Rodolphe's farewell letter after spilling the apricots under which it was hidden, she looks down upon the glittering paving-stones in the square below, and she hears the *ronflement* (the humming sound) of Binet's lathe.

> The luminous ray that rose directly from below drew the weight of her body toward the abyss. It seemed to her that the ground of the square rose oscillating along the walls, and that the floor was tipping at the end, like a pitching ship. She stood at the very edge, almost suspended, surrounded by a great space. The blue of the sky invaded her, the air circulated in her head that had become hollow, she had only to give way, to let herself be taken; and the humming [*ronflement*] of the lathe continued without a break, like a furious voice calling her.

In the last phrase the words *comme une voix furieuse* might be interpreted to suggest "like the voice of a Fury." At all events, since the sound of the lathe is likened to the sound of a voice, there is another grim link here with the echoing voices surrounding Emma's fate. And Flaubert himself tells us that when Charles' shout breaks the spell in the voice of the lathe and calls Emma back to herself, "the idea that she had just escaped death almost made her faint from terror."

The third major symbol — the Blind Beggar — we have already considered in some detail along with the terrible sound of his voice trailing away into the night. It remains now to show how the three symbols come together at last in Emma's death.

When Léon fails to obtain the money Emma needs to pay Lheureux, she visits the notary, Maître Guillaumin, who is secretly allied with Emma's creditors. He tries to make love to her, as we have seen earlier, and Emma, repulsing him, goes next to M. Binet, the tax-collector.

> He was alone, in his garret, busy imitating in wood one of those indescribable ivory pieces, made of crescents, of spheres hollowed one inside the other, the whole straight as an obelisk and of no possible use; and he was beginning the last part, he was nearing the end! In the shadowy light of the workshop, the light-colored dust flew from his machine, like a plume of sparks under the shod hooves of a galloping horse; the two wheels were turning, were humming [*ronflaient*]; Binet was smiling, his chin sunk down, his nostrils open. . . .

Binet is embarrassed at Emma's request for help and falls back before her entreaties as if he had seen a serpent. Emma rushes out then toward the cemetery and goes on to Mother Rollet's.

The nurse unlaces her and she falls sobbing on the bed. When Emma remains silent, Mother Rollet, rather strangely, goes to her spinning wheel and begins to spin flax. But Emma calls to her to stop, for she confuses the sound of the spinning wheel with the sound of Binet's lathe — and Flaubert is clearly telling us something here.

Then, lying on her back, Emma sees a long spider walking above her head in the cleft of a beam. I thought of this grim symbol some years ago when I was reading Shakespeare's *The Winter's Tale* and came upon the strange phrase: "I have drunk, and seen the spider" (II. i. 45). The words relate to the belief current in Shakespeare's time that if one drank a spider without seeing it, no harm would come of it, but if one saw the spider it would result in one's death. We have been told earlier of the silent spider ennui, spinning its web in the shadow in every corner of Emma's heart.

But it was not visible to her then. On the nurse's bed, looking up at the ceiling, Emma sees the spider for the first time. And soon thereafter, rebuffed by Rodolphe, she commits suicide, as we have seen, with arsenic from the blue bowl in Homais' pharmacy.

Emma's death is described in painful detail. When the priest brings the crucifix before administering extreme unction, the dying Emma gives to the body of the Man-God "with all her failing strength the greatest kiss of love that she had ever given." Here again we may recall the pathetic symbol of Emma's longing in the ripe fruit on the espalier waiting for a hand to take it. Then, for a moment after she has received the sacrament Emma's face has a look of serenity. But soon the terrible symptoms continue and the death-rattle grows louder.

Suddenly the sound of heavy wooden shoes is heard and the sound of a stick. Then a raucous voice rises singing familiar words:

> "Often the warmth of a fair day
> Makes a young girl dream of love."

Emma rises like a galvanized corpse, her hair disheveled, her eyes fixed and staring. The song continues, and there is a scythe in it. Emma cries out, "The Blind Man!" And she begins to laugh, an atrocious, despairing laugh as she thinks she sees the Blind Man's hideous face rising up like an ultimate horror in the eternal shadows.

Finally we hear the end of the Blind Man's Song, which Flaubert said came from Restif de la Bretonne, but which reminds me very ironically of the ballad of "Lady Isabel and the Elf-Knight."

> "The wind blew very hard that day
> And the short skirt blew away!"

Emma is shaken by a final convulsion, and when those in the room approach her she is dead.

Later, as Emma lies on her deathbed, there is a sort of white dust on her lashes, and her eyes begin to disappear in a viscous pallor as if spiders had spun a delicate web over them. We have seen earlier the light-colored dust flying from Binet's lathe during Emma's visit to his workshop. And the spider web over her eyes is clearly the work of the silent spider ennui that appeared early in the book, "spinning its web in the shadow in every corner of her heart." And so the spider and the Man with the Lathe and the Blind Man are all brought together finally for the first and only time at Emma's death.

When Emma is dressed for burial in her bridal gown and veil and satin slippers, the attendants raise her head a little to put on her crown, and then "a flood of black liquids" comes out of her mouth. Here for Emma the terrible pattern of echoes seems to have run its full course. For just as the cries of Hippolyte ("like the far-off howling of some beast being murdered") when his gangrenous leg was amputated are in a sense an antiphonal echo to what Emma had thought was the voice of happiness and prepare one for the final resolution in the voice of the Blind Man's song, so the black liquid oozing from the gangrene prepares one for the black liquids that pour from Emma's dead mouth. And the black liquid itself provides a further meaning in this echoing world. In a sense (as one of my students has suggested) the leg rotting in the horrible confinement of the intricate boxlike mechanism that Charles Bovary had constructed for Hippolyte's operation echoes the dark corridor with the locked door in which Emma Bovary has rotted away. And the black liquids are quite literally (in addition to being results of arsenic poisoning) the "black bile" of the mortal *melancholy* that we saw in another form in the web that the silent spider ennui had spun and left finally over her dead eyes. And this last suggests the spinning Fate, Clotho — just as the dust on Emma's lashes from the Lathe of Binet (who has his own measuring rod) suggests Lachesis, the Second Fate, the measurer of the thread of life — and just as the scythe in the Blind Man's song suggests Atropos, the third Fate, the unswerving one that cannot be moved, the Fate that cuts the thread of life, or Death itself. * All three of the Fates (the Greek Moirai) go back to the idea of Moira, the fated order of things beyond man's understanding, and thus provide ultimately a meaning for poor Charles Bovary's statement that Rodolphe found so banal but which, according to Flaubert, was the

---

* In relation to the hunger motif, note the eerie details that before Emma dies Binet puts up his dinner hour and complains of terrible hunger pangs, and that the Blind Man howls like a hungry dog. At Emma's wake there is the howling of a dog outside. The hunger of the Fates and Death is never satisfied.

only great phrase that Charles had ever spoken: "C'est la faute de la fatalité." It is the fault of Fate.

So the Spider and the dust and the Man with the Lathe and the Blind Man and the voices and the wind all come together in their terrible inescapable pattern of meaning, and we can see that the echoes in Emma's fate were indeed echoes in a dark corridor — a place of no exit except in death. Flaubert had written of Charles' first wife, Héloïse: "She was dead. What a surprise!" He wrote more grimly of Emma: "Elle n'existait plus," with a chilling use of the imperfect tense, which I suppose can best be understood to mean "She wasn't existing any more" — as if a watch had stopped. Finally, one may recall Flaubert's strangely ambiguous phrase after the death of Charles himself: "They opened him and found nothing." I find no further meaning for us here.

There is a passage in Flaubert's correspondence that may be recalled now at the last:

> The melancholy of antiquity seems ... more profound than that of the moderns, all of whom more or less conceive of immortality beyond the *black void* [le *trou noir*]. But, for the ancients this black void was the infinite itself: their dreams are outlined and occur against a background of immutable ebony.

Flaubert's art gave meaning to his life; but in *Madame Bovary* he seems to have brought back the immutable ebony background of the ancient world and even to have enhanced its darkness by the addition of his own nineteenth-century despair.

III

GÉRARD DE NERVAL AND THE DREAM GATES OF IVORY AND OF HORN

THE DREAM GATES first appear in the surviving literature of the West in the Fourth Book of the *Odyssey,* where they are cited in relation to the dreams of Penelope when "sweet sleep" comes to her at last in her worry over her husband's absence and the depredations of the suitors and the dangers to her son. Here the goddess Athena sends a phantom to reassure Penelope as she sleeps at last quietly "at the gates of dreams." In the Nineteenth Book the dream gates appear again when Penelope, not yet recognizing Odysseus, tells him of a dream she has had and of her wondering as to its meaning. Odysseus offers an interpretation; but Penelope is not convinced and replies to his words:

> "Stranger, dreams are truly baffling and their meaning is not clear, nor do they at all find fulfilment in all things for men. For there are two gates of shadowy dreams, and one is made of horns and one of ivory. The dreams that pass through the gate cut from ivory deceive men, bringing words without fulfilment. But those that come forth through the gate of polished horns bring true issues to pass, when any mortal sees them. But in my case, I think, it was not from there that my strange dream came." (XIX. 560-569) *

A book published in 1940 by Ernest Leslie Highbarger on *The Gates of Dreams* traces the development of this concept in Classical

---

* Translation adapted from the Loeb edition by A. T. Murray.

letters and seeks to discover its most ancient sources. Professor
Highbarger cites the recurrence of the dream gates in Plato's *Char-
mides,* where reference (as in Homer) is to the Gate of the Horns
in the plural and to the Gate of Ivory in the singular; and he
adds:

> Strictly speaking, then, the one is the Gate of the
> Horns, the other is the Gate of Ivory with the meaning
> that its two leaves *(fores)* were imagined to be made of
> ivory. This study will attempt to show that the distinction
> is deliberate and reflects a long historical development in
> which the concept 'Gates of Dreams' is derived from
> remote antiquity going back ultimately, it would appear,
> to the 'Gates of the Sky' of Egyptian and Mesopotamian
> religious belief.

Highbarger further identifies the Gate of the Horns as the Gate of
Hades, the Gate of Night and the Gate of the Dead — and
the Gate of Ivory as "the 'Gate of Olympus' . . . through which the
gods come and go and through which dreams are often sent to
men on earth by the gods." In the Sixth Book of the *Aeneid,* Aeneas
returns from the underworld by the Gate of Ivory, and Highbarger
sees him and the Sibyl as clearly having entered by the same gate.

Ultimately the dream gates seem to go back to Eastern ideas
of the gates of life and death. Highbarger finds a "Gate of the
Horns" and a "Gate of the East" in Egyptian thought and in
Mesopotamian art, and he concludes that . . .

> The Gate of the Horns in Homer, Plato and Vergil
> alike is derived, therefore, ultimately from Egyptian or
> Mesopotamian eschatology, possibly from both. It is the
> Gate of the West, or the entrance to the realm of ghosts.
> In sharp contrast to this, the Gate of the East was the
> place of the rising sun, who symbolized life, happiness,
> and all that is bright. From the earliest times a considerable
> degree of poetry grew up about this latter Gate, and from
> its lyric associations the Greeks finally developed the Gate
> of Ivory, which likewise suggested the east and the realm of
> life.

All this seems to leave considerable ambiguity still as to the
ideas behind the routing of the true and false dreams cited by

Penelope; but it suggests the ancient roots below the image of the dream gates and the lasting imaginative power in the archetypal symbol of the gateways for life and death and the passage for the various dreams of men.

In the Renaissance, in Chapter XIII of *Le tiers livre* Rabelais offers an explanation drawn from Macrobius of the dream-gates of Homer and Vergil; and in the early period of French Romanticism Mme de Staël refers to the Ivory Dream Gate in her study *Of Germany*. But the most notable modern reference is in the opening paragraph of Gérard de Nerval's *Aurélia, or Dream and Life,* which introduces us at once into the mysterious regions where the real and the imagined worlds intermingle to provide for certain questing minds like Nerval's another dimension of psychic experience.

We shall see something of all this in various aspects of the present paper, in which I shall try to provide glimpses into the life and mind and writings of a strangely beautiful spirit of the last century who seems to me to have a special significance and interest for our time.

* * *

In the person of Gérard Labrunie (1808-1855), who called himself Gérard de Nerval, French Romanticism affords us one of its most gracious and most tragic figures. Known in his lifetime as a minor writer of the Romantic movement, "le bon Gérard" was recognized for the charm of his personality, for his eccentricities, for his recurrent mental illness that brought him on several occasions to the asylum, and for his varied writings, none of which at the time was thought to assure him a very significant place in literature. It is noteworthy in this regard that the 18th edition of Gustave Lanson's classic history of French literature in 1924, in all of its 1266 pages has no mention of Gérard except for six lines in part of a footnote that cites him admiringly, but primarily for his translation of Goethe's *Faust*. Yet today, over a century after his death, thanks in part to Proust and the Surrealists, Gérard de Nerval is considered one of the major figures of French Romanticism and receives more critical attention than any other French Romantic poet except Hugo.

It has been remarked by recent critics that Nerval is the nearest in spirit of all the French Romantics to the poets of German Romanticism; and his attraction to Goethe and Novalis and Jean-Paul and Hoffmann and his friendship with Heine are all evidence of this deep affiliation. Moreover, as we shall see, Nerval had a profoundly personal attachment to Germany, for his mother was buried there.

A few details of his life are a necessary prelude to any discussion of the major writings and significance of Gérard de Nerval. The son of Etienne Labrunie and Marie-Antoinette-Marguerite Laurent, Gérard was born of "a woman of the North" and "a man of the South" — his mother's family coming from Picardy and the region of the Ile de France and his father's from the Agenais region with recollections for Gérard of Périgord and the Dordogne. But Gérard liked to imagine himself of nobler ancestry and drew his pseudonym *de Nerval* from a plot of land supposedly associated with the Roman Emperor Nerva; and near the end of his life he put together a genealogical chart attempting to show that on his father's side he was descended from three lords of Labrunie who were knights under the Emperor Otto.

Gérard's father was a doctor with the Grande Armée and served with the Army of the Rhine. His mother accompanied her husband and died in Germany in November of 1810 when her son was still in infancy. She was buried there in the Polish Catholic cemetery of Gross-Glogau. Gérard spent his early years with his great-uncle Antoine Boucher at Mortefontaine, where he may have read rather widely in his relative's strange collection of esoteric books. He was never close to his father; but the mother he had never known was apparently to become a major psychological influence in his life. In 1820 he was living with his father and attending the Lycée Charlemagne in Paris, where Théophile Gautier was one of his schoolmates. Publication of minor poems in 1826 was followed in 1828 by his famous translation of the first part of Goethe's *Faust*. He met Victor Hugo and became one of the lively young Romantics of the day; and he took part in the famous *première* of *Hernani,* so enthusiastically described in Gautier's *History of Romanticism.*

At his grandfather's death Gérard inherited a small fortune which enabled him to travel in the south of France and in Italy.

Then he met Jenny Colon, a young actress at the Variétés, and used up the rest of his inheritance on the *Monde Dramatique,* a journal devoted to the theatre in which he had hoped to further Jenny's career. This was the happy time of life for the young Romantics in the famous Impasse du Doyenné adjacent to the Louvre; but Gérard was soon to find himself in debt. In the spring of 1838 Jenny Colon married a flute player, and in the late summer Nerval set out for Germany. He had become increasingly fascinated with the theatre and hoped for great success in drama. All the rest of his life he was to pursue this elusive dream, which is thought by some of his biographers to have been in part responsible for his death.

In February of 1841 Gérard suffered his first mental attack and was taken to a *maison de santé* on the rue Picpus. A month later another crisis led to an eight-month stay in Dr. Esprit Blanche's asylum on Montmartre. The following year Jenny Colon died and at the year's end Gérard set out for the East where he travelled to Malta, Alexandria, Cairo, Beyruth, Smyrna, and Constantinople He continued writing and traveling and had hopes of success in the theatre. In 1849, 1850, 1851 and 1852 he suffered from illness or depression. Early in 1853 he worked on *Sylvie* and spent nearly two months in the *maison Dubois.* On August 15, *Sylvie* appeared in the *Revue des Deux Mondes,* and less than a fortnight later Gérard was in Dr. Emile Blanche's establishment at Passy for treatment. At the end of September he was released too soon and suffered a relapse. In October he was back with Dr. Blanche and before the year was out had finished *Les Filles du Feu* and *Les Chimères.*

In the spring of 1854 Gérard left the asylum and set out for Germany, where it is likely that he visited his mother's grave in the Glogau cemetery. At all events, he suffered another serious relapse, and early in August, after his return, was back with Dr. Blanche and working on *Aurélia, or Dream and Life.* In mid-autumn he was unwisely released at the intervention of well-meaning friends.

The last days of Gérard's life, as we shall see later, form a strange and harrowing part of what has since become the Nerval legend. In the ensuing pages we shall examine in particular three of

Gérard's finest writings — *Sylvie, Les Chimères,* and *Aurélia* — and attempt to capture from them some of the elements that make Nerval so fascinating a figure in French and western letters.

* * *

Already in a few of Nerval's early poems such as "Fantaisie" and "Les Cydalises" we find the lovely, nostalgic note that is peculiarly his own. In "Fantaisie" Gérard tells of a tune that he prefers to anything by Rossini, Mozart or Weber — "a tune very old, languishing and sad, which for me has secret charms!" When he hears it, two hundred years roll away and he finds himself in the time of Louis XIII before a brick château in great parks, with a river flowing among flowers. Then at a high window he sees a fair-haired lady with dark eyes, dressed in a costume of those ancient days — a lady, he writes, "whom I have already seen, perhaps, in another existence . . . and whom I remember!"

The second poem, "Les Cydalises," is so musical and delicate that there is probably nothing of the sort comparable in French letters before Verlaine. There is no possibility of translating it successfully into another tongue; but let me give you the literal sense as best I can in prose and then read you the verses as Nerval wrote them. The word *cydalises* in the plural we can perhaps best translate here as "the women who loved us."

> Where are those who loved us?
> They are in the grave:
> They are happier,
> In a fairer place!
>
> They are near the angels,
> In the depths of the blue sky,
> And sing the praises
> Of the Mother of God!
>
> O white fiancée!
> O young maiden in flower!
> Wearied lover,
> Whom sorrow withered!
>
> Deep eternity
> Used to smile in your eyes . . .
> Torches put out by the world,
> Be lighted again in heaven!

And in Gérard's own words:

Les Cydalises

Où sont nos amoureuses?
Elles sont au tombeau:
Elles sont plus heureuses,
Dans un séjour plus beau!

Elles sont près des anges,
Dans le fond du ciel bleu,
Et chantent les louanges
De la mère de Dieu!

O blanche fiancée!
O jeune vierge en fleur!
Amante délaissée,
Que flétrit la douleur!

L'éternité profonde
Souriait dans vos yeux . . .
Flambeaux éteints du monde,
Rallumez-vous aux cieux!

Gérard de Nerval loved the beautiful Valois country northeast of Paris and its old songs and legends, and when he writes of this region there is something in his style, as Marcel Proust once observed, that is not in the words or in what is said — "*it is entirely between the words,* like the mist of a morning at Chantilly." One of the most exquisite of Gérard's writings is concerned with this region — *Sylvie, Souvenirs du Valois (Memories of the Valois Region);* and in its pages we can find at once something of the innocent grace and the human loneliness and ineptitude for ordinary life and loving that are part of Gérard's essential character.

Andrew Lang wrote of *Sylvie* that "it is one of the little masterpieces of the world. It has a Greek perfection. One reads it, and however old one is, youth comes back, and April. . . ." It seems to me that this is so; for I find in *Sylvie* something of the fresh beauty of the ancient pastoral — the beauty of Theocritus or of *Daphnis and Chloe* that belongs to eternal springtime. And yet there is the seed of sorrow in *Sylvie,* for it reflects the qualities of Nerval's mind that would keep him always from commitments to the loving of this world.

Sylvie is part of Gérard's volume called *Les Filles du Feu (Daughters of the Fire),* and I do not know quite what he meant to convey by the inclusive title. In Emerson's Second Series of Essays (published in 1844) there is a passage in his lecture on "The Poet" that may be pertinent here. I have no knowledge that Nerval had read the essay; but one will notice among the authors and mystics cited several that Gérard has referred to with deep sympathy. According to Emerson

> . . . the highest minds of the world have never ceased to explore the double meaning, or shall I say the quadruple or the centuple or much more manifold meaning, of every sensuous fact; Orpheus, Empedocles, Heraclitus, Plato, Plutarch, Dante, Swedenborg, and the masters of sculpture, picture and poetry. For we are not pans and barrows, nor even porters of the fire and torch-bearers, but children of the fire, made of it, and only the same divinity transmuted and at two or three removes, when we know least about it.

In *Sylvie* there are no very sombre tones; but there is a note of sadness, as we have suggested earlier, and there is a brief shadow from an age of doubt that is symptomatic of the anguish that will appear later in *Aurélia. Sylvie* is not perhaps literally Gérard's autobiography; but the states of mind depicted there and the general situations mirror his nature so clearly that I shall not try to distinguish between fact and fancy in my paper.

In the first section Gérard tells how he has been going nightly to the theatre for a year to admire on the stage in mediocre plays in actress who seems to him, under the lights, to sum up all that is ideal in woman. He has learned from an uncle that nature has forgotten to make hearts for actresses; but he smilingly assumes that this must refer to those of the past century. Then he analyses briefly the strange era in which he was living — an age like those that ordinarily follow revolutions or the decline from eras of great rulers. The heroic love affairs of the Fronde were gone and likewise the elegant vice of the Regency and the scepticism and orgies of the Directory. The new era was confused — in Gérard's words:

...it was a mixture of activity, hesitation and idleness, of brilliant utopias, philosophic or religious aspirations, and vague enthusiasms, mingled with certain instincts of rebirth....

Nerval sees it as being something like the era of Apuleius, whose *Golden Ass* was to influence his conception of the great Mother Goddess; and he adds, in reference to Apuleius's book:

Material man longed for the bouquet of roses that was to effect his regeneration at the hands of the beautiful Isis; the goddess eternally young and pure appeared to us in the nights and made us ashamed of the daylight hours we had lost.

Nerval depicts himself and his fellows as without any ambition for the positions and honors characteristic of the age and as seeking refuge from the crowd in the poet's ivory tower, where they lived apart intoxicated with poetry and love. But the love was vague, made up of metaphysical ghosts. "Seen close at hand," says Nerval, "real woman revolted our innocence! she had to appear as queen or goddess, and most of all had to be kept at a distance."

In his ensuing relationships with women, as we see them in his finest work, Gérard seems never for long to have forgotten this precept. It is as if he were convinced that any dreams he might have had of loving a woman in this world must have come to him through the ivory dream gate, the entryway provided for false dreams. And thus, when an acquaintance points out to him an apparently successful rival for his actress's affection, Gérard looks at him and says, "What does it matter to me whether it is he or someone else? There had to be someone, and that one seems to me worthy of having been chosen." —"But what about you?" his friend asks. —"Me? I pursued an image, nothing more." And when a lucky turn of investments noted in the newspaper makes Nerval suddenly rich for the moment and he thinks how he could replace the fortunate lover, his pride revolts: "No! it is not thus at my age that one kills love with gold. I shall not corrupt anyone. Moreover this is an idea from another era...." And he turns to look vaguely at the newspaper and sees the announcement of a festival he had known in his youth: "Festival of the Bouquet in the provinces. —Tomorrow the archers of Senlis must return the bouquet to those of Loisy." And the simple words recall to Nerval a long-forgotten memory:

> ... The horn and the drum were resounding far away in the hamlets and the woods: the young girls fashioned garlands and as they sang they sorted out bouquets adorned with ribbons. —A heavy cart, drawn by oxen, received their presents as it passed by, and we, children of these country regions, formed the procession with our bows and our arrows, decorating ourselves with the title of knights, — without realizing that we were only repeating from age to age a druidic festival, outlasting the monarchies and the new religions.

Gérard could not sleep that night. All his youth came back in memories and he recalled another festival he had attended years before when he was young. He saw once more a château of the time of Henry IV surrounded by green lawns and framed in elms and lindens, and the late sunlight shining through their leaves. And he writes of it:

> Young girls were dancing in a circle on the grass and singing old songs handed down by their mothers, and in a French so naturally pure that one felt himself to be living in that old Valois region, where the heart of France has been beating for over a thousand years.

For some reason Gérard was the only boy in this circle of dancers to which he had brought his young companion Sylvie. Until that moment he had had eyes only for her and loved no one but her. He had hardly noticed among the others a tall, beautiful, blond girl named Adrienne. Then suddenly he and Adrienne were together in the middle of the circle and had to embrace as the dancers turned more swiftly around them. It was a fatal moment for Gérard...

> As I kissed her, I could not keep from pressing her hand. The long ringlets of her golden hair brushed my cheeks. From that moment, a strange confusion possessed me that I had not known before.

Then, according to the ritual, Adrienne had to sing in order to reenter the dance. The description of her song explains why Nerval was in thrall thereafter to her memory:

We sat down around her, and at once, with a fresh and penetrating voice, slightly husky, like that of the girls of this misty region, she sang one of those ancient songs full of melancholy and love, that tell forever of the miseries of a princess shut up in a tower at the will of a father who punishes her for having loved. . . .

As she sang darkness descended from the great trees, and the rising moonlight fell on her alone, set off from our attentive circle. —She stopped singing, and no one dared break the silence. The lawn was covered with frail condensed vapors, which unfolded their white flakes on the tips of the grass. We thought we were in paradise.

Gérard rises and gets a laurel crown tied with a ribbon and places it on Adrienne's head where it shines in the pale moonlight on her blond hair. She seems to him to resemble Dante's Beatrice, smiling at him on the threshold of heaven. Then Adrienne rises, bows gracefully, and runs back into the château. Gérard learns that she is descended from a family allied to the ancient kings of France — that she has the blood of the Valois in her veins. She had been allowed to be present for once at this local festival; but they would not see her again, for she was returning the next day to her convent school.

Gérard remembers all this as he thinks of going back to see the provincial festival again. He remembers how Sylvie had cried because he had given the crown to Adrienne — and how he had brought back to Paris "this double image of a tender friendship sadly broken — and of an impossible vague love, the source of sorrowful thoughts that school philosophy had no power to calm." At vacation time the following year he learns that Adrienne is destined to be a nun.

Already in Gérard's mind we find the shifting visions in which those he thinks he loves will merge. He comments on it in *Sylvie,* as he considers returning for the ancient festival:

Everything was explained for me by this memory that was half a dream. This vague and hopeless love for a woman of the theatre which seized possession of me every evening at the hour of the play and did not leave me until I fell asleep, had its source in the memory of Adrienne, a flower of the night that had opened in the pale light of the moon, a fair and rosy phantom gliding over the green grass half bathed in white vapors.

The figure of Adrienne, apparently forgotten for years, comes back sharply to Gérard's mind, and he cries out: "To think of loving a nun under the form of an actress! . . . and suppose she were the same person! —It is enough to drive one mad! a fatal attraction of the unknown like the will-o'-the-wisp that flees away over the reeds of a stagnant pond . . . But let us get back to reality." And he wonders why he has forgotten Sylvie for the past three years. She will still be there — good and pure of heart — still waiting for him, since she is too poor to be married.

He recalls the last time he had returned to Loisy. He had found Sylvie more beautiful than ever, and he had placed a fair crown on her head in atonement for hurting her by failing to do so before. This time everything went well. Everything favored him, and he was thinking only of Sylvie. But when he saw a convent it occurred to him for a moment that perhaps it was Adrienne's.

In one charming scene during this episode the two young people visit Sylvie's widowed aunt and put on the clothes worn long before by the aunt and her husband on their wedding day. "We were the bride and groom," writes Nerval, "for the whole of one fair summer morning." But, in witnessing a sort of mummer's play thereafter, Gérard half fancies that he sees Adrienne in the form of a spirit rising from the abyss with a flaming sword.

Nerval recalls all this as he goes in the coach along the Plessis way *en route* once again to the ball at Loisy. This time Sylvie seems distant. She tells him that the last time he came he was Saint-Preux for her and that she saw herself as Julie. Why didn't he come back then? They told her he was in Italy. At last, in tears, he confesses his irresolutions and his whims, and pleads with her to save him. But they are interrupted, and the opportunity is lost. Later Sylvie sings for him one of the old songs that he loves:

> A Dammartin l'y a trois belles filles:
> L'y en a z'une plus belle que le jour. . . .

He learns soon after that Sylvie is probably going to be married to *le grand frisé* (Big Curly-Head), a peasant friend of his childhood who is about to set up a pastry shop at Dammartin. Gérard does not wait any longer. He returns to Paris the next day.

Later he brings his actress from Paris to the place where he had met Adrienne, and he tells her the whole story of the source of his love for her. But the actress says, "You do not love me. You expected me to say: 'The actress and the nun are one and the same person'; you are merely seeking a drama, and the dénouement eludes you. Come, I don't believe you any more." And later she points out her leading man to Gérard and says: "There is the one who loves me!"

Finally, Gérard tells of a later visit to Sylvie at Dammartin. She was married then to *le grand frisé* and had two lively children. And at the last he recalls that he had once taken Sylvie to see his actress put on a play at Dammartin and had asked if she did not see in her some resemblance to Adrienne. Sylvie had laughed at the idea. Then, turning serious, she had sighed and said: "Poor Adrienne! she died in the convent... about 1832."

* * *

We have suggested earlier the remarkable influence exerted upon Gérard by the dead mother he had never known. She seems to have played a dominant role in Gérard's conception of woman and thus to have entered into his ineffectual search for ideal love. It seems clear also that she determines in part the direction of Gérard's religious longing, which moves primarily toward the female saints and the great Mother Goddess in all her variant forms.

Gérard, like many another of his time, had lost his religious faith under the influence of eighteenth-century thought; but he had not lost his longing, and religious preoccupations have a major role in much of what he writes. In earlier lectures we have shown the strange dilemma in which man finds himself when (like Baudelaire) he keeps a sense of relationship with eternity but has little hope of salvation, and the peculiar emptiness in man's existence when (like Flaubert) he is at heart a mystic and believes in nothing. In Gérard de Nerval we see an essentially religious mind struggling (as many have done since) to find a substitute for lost faith. With Gérard this struggle entailed creation of a sort of personal myth and the employment of a mass of esoteric details from undisciplined readings in many forms of religious and occult literature. There is a peculiar fascination in what comes of this, for Gérard was a marvellously gifted poet with an ability unparalleled in French letters to combine details from his personal experience with archetypal and mythical and esoteric reference; and this, in combination with the strange logic that persisted even in his madness, helps to give his writing its unique quality and power.

This is nowhere more evident than in the twelve densely written sonnets of *Les Chimères,* which Gérard published as part of *Les Filles du Feu* in January, 1854. Gérard himself wrote to his friend Dumas that the poems of *Les Chimères* were composed "in that state of revery which the Germans would call *supernaturalistic";* and he added that "they are hardly more obscure than the metaphysics of Hegel or Swedenborg's *Memorabilia,* and would lose their charm in being explained, if that were possible." Needless to say, explicators have been trying to explain them ever since.

It is perhaps worth noting that seven of the original twelve sonnets of *Les Chimères* had appeared earlier in Gérard's *Petits Châteaux de Bohème* of 1853 under the collective title *Mysticisme.* The title is of interest in that one finds ancient deities in some of the sonnets and a five-poem sequence called "Le Christ aux Oliviers" with an epigraph from Jean-Paul saying that "God is dead!" I doubt that a mystic would sense in any of these poems the presence of his God.

For my purpose this evening, I shall examine only three of the sonnets of *Les Chimères* — "Vers dorés," "Horus," and "Artémis" — the first in order to suggest something of the nature of Gérard's pantheistic esotericism, and the other two to show how the changing and shifting and intermingling figures of the women in Gérard's dreams are paralleled by the changing and shifting and intermingling figures of his saints and gods.

The sonnet called "Vers dorés "("Golden Verses") takes from Pythagoras its title and its epigraph: "Eh quoi! tout est sensible!" ("Everything feels!") The magic and strange power of Nerval's poetry are necessarily lost in translation; but I have tried to keep at least the literal meaning of the original verses to suggest the mysterious sense of life that Gérard has put into the heart of his poem:

Free-thinking man! do you believe that you alone are thinking
In this world where life bursts forth in everything?
Your freedom controls the powers that you hold,
But from all your councils the universe is absent.

Respect in the beast a spirit in action:
Each flower is a soul that has opened to Nature;
A mystery of love lies at rest in the metal;
"Everything feels!" And everything has power over your being.

Fear, in the blind wall, a gaze that spies upon you.
A word is attached even to matter . . .
Don't make it serve any impious usage!

Often in the obscure being there dwells a God concealed,
And, like an eye being born covered by its lids,
A pure spirit grows under the bark of the stones!

In such a world one can understand the preoccupations of a sensitive and often deranged mind like Nerval's with the fearful possibilities in correspondences. Under the influence of such a belief every object is full of mystery and linked with a greater mystery. But one can hardly see it in itself as providing much more than a sort of cosmic thrill.

The second sonnet, "Horus," is an example of Nerval's religious syncretism, in which the ancient gods seem to flow into each other and dissolve and reflect, as in a sort of vanishing and recurring echo, the gods that are gone and those that are yet to come. The names of deities and mythic reference and familiar symbols intermingle and change and fade in what seems to be a hymn to the life-giving force in the great Mother Goddess and the new god about to be born.

The god Kneph trembling shook the universe:
Isis, the mother, then rose on her couch,
Made a gesture of hatred to her fierce husband,
And the ardor of former days burned in her green eyes.

"Do you see him?" she said. "That perverse old creature is dying,
All the frosts in the world have passed over his mouth,
Tie up his twisted foot, put out his squinting eye,
He is the god of volcanoes and the king of winters!

The eagle has already passed, the new spirit calls me,
I have put on for him the dress of Cybele [the great Mother
He is the beloved child of Hermes and Osiris!"   [Goddess] . . .

The goddess had fled on her golden conch-shell,
The sea sent back to us her adored image,
And the skies shone under the scarf of Iris [the rainbow].

Many explanations have been suggested for the details of this poem, which has been given, among others, an alchemical interpretation. But beyond all such esoteric references, the verses clearly reflect the religious syncretism of Nerval — his attempt to adapt even the gods into a continuing pattern of birth and death and rebirth in terms of the great force of Life in the universe.

One will note here, for example, at the death of one god (Kneph) anticipation of the birth of another (Horus). The image of the flying eagle seems, among other possible meanings, to pre-figure the seer's insight (the eagle of St. John on Patmos, for ex-ample — *Johannis aquila*) and to provide another link with Chris-tian iconography. Thus, the whole poem is Nerval's statement of the survival of the great life-force in the universe, seen in terms of nascent and dying religions and their gods. Isis assumes the form of Cybele, the Great Mother Goddess, to bring forth the new god Horus; and she flees from the old god (who is so "perverse" as to die) in the form of Aphrodite-Venus on a golden conch-shell under the rainbow, God's promise in the sky, the symbol of the Virgin Mary and the Christ to come. In the first quatrain of the sonnet in French there is even a very strange pattern, unique in Nerval's verses, in which the first and last letters of each line spell in turn in English, as I have suggested elsewhere, what seems to me the essential meaning of the poem: "LIFE SEES!"

In the third sonnet, "Artémis," the metamorphoses and shifting identities appear to be related more immediately to human ref-erence; but the gods and the saints are included, and Jean Richer (while admitting the extreme importance of the biographical sense) would interpret the poem largely in terms of an illustration of the goddess Isis from Athanasius Kircher's *Oedipus Aegyptiacus,* with details derived from *The Golden Ass* of Apuleius. At all events, one can see in the verses the shifting, changing forms of mortal love as well as of female saints and gods; and the poem is not only a remarkable analysis in the psychology of human relationships, but a peculiarly vivid example of the fluid and interpenetrating and

interchanging elements in Gérard's own recollections of the women
he has loved and of his linking them with saints and deities:

The Thirteenth comes again . . . It is still the first;
And it is always the only one — or the only moment;
For are you queen, O you! the first or the last?
Are you king, you the only or the last lover? . . .

Love the one who loved you from the cradle into the grave;
She whom I alone loved loves me still tenderly:
It is death — or the dead woman . . . O delight! O torment!
The rose that she holds is the *Rose trémière* [the holyhock].

Neapolitan saint with your hands full of fire,
Rose with the violet heart, flower of Saint Gudule:
Have you found your cross in the wilderness of the skies?

White roses, fall! you insult our gods,
Fall, white phantoms, from your burning sky:
—The saint of the abyss is more holy in my eyes!

In this strange world one senses the longings of Gérard — human
and spiritual — and the lack of any clear spiritual commitment.
As Jean Richer has written earlier, it is not a mystic writing — one
might say, rather, a dreamer, who has fashioned for himself a
dream world of phantoms that have come through the ivory dream
gate of insubstantial dreams.

Yet, even in his strangest fantasies and in his madness, Gérard's
mind kept an impressive logical subtlety and precision in details,
as is evident in the famous anecdote of the lobster that Gérard
took for a stroll on a blue ribbon under the galleries of the Palais
Royal. Gautier tells of the incident in an article he wrote about
Gérard on the Day of the Dead (November 2, 1867), nearly
thirteen years after Nerval's death. According to Gautier, Gérard's
defense of his strange companion was as follows:

> "In what way is a lobster more ridiculous than a dog,
> a cat, a gazelle, a lion or any other beast that one drags
> after him? I have a taste for lobsters, which are calm,
> serious, know the secrets of the sea, and don't bark and
> swallow the human monad like dogs. . . ."

I have tried to show in another publication that there is an eerie
logic in this passage, inspired in Gérard's strange mind, as I see

it, by the card called "The Moon" — the 18th card of the Greater Arcana — in the Tarot pack. Anyone who has examined the Tarot will realize how rich the cards are in what we have come to call archetypal images. The Moon Card is peculiarly memorable. It shows the moon (which Gérard associated with Isis) raining down a mysterious dew. Strange towers frame the background horizon, and beneath the moon two dogs (or a dog and a wolf), looking upward, seem to be barking at or swallowing the lunar emanations. Beneath, in the center of the illustration at the bottom, is the figure of a lobster-crab, nearly as large as the dogs, rising from the waters, apparently drawn upward by the moon's magnetic powers. Gérard must have been familiar with this illustration in Court de Gebelin's *Monde primitif,* which Jean Richer has identified as "a constant source" for his writing; and if it inspired his memorable stroll with a lobster on a blue ribbon (blue — "the color of the Sea" according to Court de Gebelin), it is only another indication of the peculiar and persistent logic, even in madness, in Nerval's disordered brain.

*　*　*

Jean Richer has traced Nerval's occultism and esotericism in a classic study (*Gérard de Nerval et les doctrines ésotériques* [1947]), which suggests the extent and complexity of Gérard's readings over the years in the great religious texts (the Bible, the Koran, the Talmud, the Zohar [in the Latin translation of Pico della Mirandola]); in the writings of mystics like Martines de Pasqually, Saint Martin, Swedenborg, and Jacob Boehme; and in the esoteric writings of the Abbé Villars, Bekker, the Abbé Tarrasson, Athanasius Kircher, Dom Pernety, and Mesmer — to mention only a few. All this forms a background for *Les Chimères,* for the strange volume entitled *Voyage en Orient,* and for Gérard's final work — the remarkable account of his dreams and his madness called *Aurélia ou le rêve et la vie (Aurélia, or Dream and Life),* which he was apparently finishing during his very last days.

In *Aurélia* the dream gates open in the first paragraph upon Nerval's inner world, as he writes:

> The Dream is a second life. I have not been able to pierce without trembling those gates of ivory or of horn

that separate us from the invisible world. The first moments of sleep are the image of death; a cloudy numbness seizes upon our thought, and we cannot determine the precise moment at which the ego, under another form, continues the work of existence. It is a vague subterranean region which lights up little by little, and in which there free themselves from the shadow and from the night the pale figures gravely motionless that inhabit the region of Limbo. Then the picture takes shape, a new light illumines and sets in motion these bizarre apparitions; — the world of the Spirits opens for us.

In the very next sentence Gérard refers to Swedenborg's *Memorabilia, The Golden Ass* of Apuleius, and *The Divine Comedy;* and in the following paragraph he sets the stage for the narrative element in *Aurélia* by calling it his *Vita nuova* and thus suggesting an immediate parallel with the early spiritual adventures of Dante.

Influenced by his great predecessors, Nerval says he will try in *Aurélia* "to transcribe the impressions of a long illness that occurred entirely in the mysteries of my mind." Yet he hesitates to use the word *illness,* for he had never felt better in his essential being — he had seemed to know everything, and his imagination had furnished him with infinite delights. "Must I regret having lost them," he asks, "in recovering what men call reason?"

Nerval then recounts the strange, broken episodes of his madness and his dreams. He had lost a lady whom he had long loved and whom he will call Aurélia. Guilty of an unpardonable offense against her (apparently infidelity), he has no hope of forgiveness. He tells of the salutation and sad glance she had given him in life after his fault — and of terrible portents he had had of her death or of his own. A strange, fallen figure in one of his dreams resembles the angel in Dürer's *Melencolia I.* As the hour he considers fatal approaches, Gérard seeks a star in the sky while he walks with a friend toward the East. He sends the friend away, saying that they belong to different heavens — that those who await him are in his star. "Here began for me," writes Gérard, "what I shall call the overflow of the dream into real life. From this moment, everything took on at times a dual aspect, — but always with a logic behind my reasoning and with my memory retaining the slightest details of what happened to me."

Gérard follows his star, alone now, singing a mysterious hymn which he seems to remember from a previous existence and scattering his earthly garments as he goes. A patrol picks him up, and he has the terrible experience of imagining his friends coming for him and taking away his *double,* while he remains behind. (The illusion of the double recurs in Nerval's *Voyage en Orient* in the tale of the Calif Hakem and elsewhere and seems to have been a subtle part of his mental illness.) He dreams later of crossing the Rhine and learns from a talking bird about members of his family living and dead. He finds himself carried along by a stream of melted metal colored by different chemicals; and he comes to realize that one's ancestors assume certain animal forms to revisit one on earth. He is filled with joy at learning that men are immortal and preserve the images of the world in which they once lived.

Then, in a dream, he crosses a threshold, in spite of the threats of its guardian, and finds himself among representatives of a strange people who bring him memories as of a lost paradise; and he rejoices in assurance that there is a God. But all this changes in an ensuing dream, where a woman he is following grows ever taller in moonlight as the whole garden in which they find themselves takes her shape, and she grows until she seems to vanish. Gérard cries out to her not to flee away, for he knows that nature will die with her. He strikes against a section of the garden wall beneath which lies the bust of a woman which seems to be of the figure he has seen. The garden takes on the appearance of a cemetery, and voices are heard crying: "The Universe is in night!"

Gérard realizes later the meaning of his dream: Aurélia is dead. He sees her in the form of a divinity, tries (in a mysterious passage) to represent the first seven Elohim who had divided the world, and is transported to an obscure planet where life is beginning. Then the monsters he has seen change form; and he finds a vast harmony (presided over by a radiant goddess), in which the birds, beasts, fish and reptiles evolve. Then the *Afrites* are created from the earth, and great combats take place under cabalistic influences. The Flood comes and the sons of Noah build a new world, while the necromancers move for a time underground.

The illusion of the double recurs, and Gérard has the horrible suspicion that Aurélia is to be given in mystic marriage to *the other* — that she is no longer his. He hears later the dolorous cry of a woman in the night — the cry of a living person, not from a dream; but for Nerval the voice is Aurélia's. At the end of the first part of his book Gérard is suffering from a terrible sense of guilt. He has troubled the harmony of the magic universe and can expect only wrath and scorn. "The irritated spirits," he writes, "fled away with cries, tracing fatal circles in the air, like birds before an approaching storm."

*   *   *

For the second part of *Aurélia* Gérard uses as an epigraph the tragic words "Euridice! Euridice!" — the cry of Orpheus "on the sheer threshold of the night." And Gérard's anguish is apparent in the opening lines: "Lost a second time! All is finished, everything done! It is I now who must die and die without hope. —What then is death? Suppose it were nothingness . . . Would to God it were! But God himself cannot make death be nothingness."

Philosophy is of no help to one "when the soul floats uncertain between life and dream" — at such a time one needs religion. But Gérard turns to his cabalistic books. He has a strange dream of a cemetery where he cannot find Aurélia's grave. A certain hour strikes and he knows it is too late. Voices answer: "She is lost!" And deep night surrounds him. He seems to see Aurélia as if by a lightning-flash "pale and dying, carried away by dark horsemen. . . ." He awakens with a cry of anguish.

Gérard recalls his youth, his mother lost in his infancy, his straying from "the true way," and his feeling of being drawn back into it by the cherished memory of a dead woman. And he adds in a phrase one may recall hereafter: "Despair and suicide are the results of certain fatal situations for one who has no faith in immortality, in its sufferings and its joys. . . ."

In a little village outside Paris he hears a woman singing near his table, and her voice recalls Aurélia's. He wonders if he can change his life. Later he sees a tall workman carrying on his left shoulder a child in a hyacinth-colored dress. He imagines it is St. Christopher with the Christ child and feels increasing guilt. He wants to confess to a priest, but the priest is of another parish and puts him off until the next day. Weeping, Gérard goes toward Notre Dame de Lorette, but something tells him that the Virgin is dead and that his prayers are useless. Above the Tuileries he thinks he sees a black sun in the empty sky and a globe red with blood. He says to himself: "The eternal night is beginning and it is going to be terrible. What will happen when men see that there is no sun any more?"

Sight of the hippopotamus in the Jardin des Plantes and of the bones of great animals in various exhibits recalls the time of the Flood. A deluge begins and Gérard throws what he apparently considers a talismanic ring into the current of waters. The storm subsides and a ray of sunlight appears. Gérard begins to hope once more. At a friend's home he falls into exhausted sleep and has a marvellous vision:

> It seemed to me that the goddess [Isis] appeared to me saying: 'I am the same as Mary, the same as your mother, the same also that under all her forms you have always loved. At each of your trials, I have put off one of the masks with which I veil my features, and soon you will see me as I am.'

Soon after, Gérard has to be taken by friends to the hospital. But he thinks he is undergoing the trials foretold by Isis in his dream. He believes he influences the motion of the moon and imagines that his role is "to reestablish universal harmony by cabalistic art and to seek a solution by evoking the occult forces of the various religions." The goddess Isis appears to him in the form of the ancient Venus and sometimes under the features of the Virgin Mary.

Finally, after he has helped a young madman with his loving sympathy, Gérard has a dream of the goddess, whose passing makes the flowers grow, and she tells him that his period of trial is over. The dawn is coming and Gérard writes on his wall: "Tu m'as visité cette nuit." ("This night you came to me.")

In scattered fragments Gérard appends, under the title *Mémorables (Memorabilia)*, the impressions of a few later dreams, and *Aurélia* ends with these words:

> ...I feel happy in my acquired convictions, and I compare this series of trials that I have endured to what, for the Ancients, was represented by the idea of a descent to the underworld.

* * *

Gérard's last days afford a sombre end to his strange life. On October 19, 1854 he had been released, obviously uncured, from the asylum of Dr. Blanche at the behest of the Committee of the Society of Men of Letters. The winter season was approaching, and when it came Nerval had no established home. He had formed the habit of walking by night around Paris, rather as Restif de la Bretonne had done the century before. Now and then he was picked up by the watch and lodged in jail. Sometimes he stayed with his Aunt Labrunie. One of his last letters, without address or date, includes verses that say he has no fire and continue:

Je vais trouver le *joint* du ciel ou de l'enfer,
Et j'ai pour l'autre monde enfin bouclé mes guêtres.

[I am going to find the *hinge* of heaven or of hell,
And I have finally buckled on my gaiters for the other world.]

There is also included the pathetic sonnet that is called his "Epitaph":

He lived, at times gay as a starling,
By turn, in love, careless and tender,
Sometimes sombre and full of dream, like a sad Clitandre.
One day he heard someone ringing at his door.

It was death! Then he asked her to wait
Until he had put a period to his last sonnet.
And then, unperturbed, he went to stretch out
In the depths of the chill coffin where his body shook with the cold.

He was an idler, as the story goes,
And let the ink dry too much in his inkwell.
He wanted to know everything, but he knew nothing at all.

And when the moment came in which, tired of this life,
One winter night finally his soul was taken from him,
He went off saying: Why did I come?

The winter nights were cold at the end of January in 1855; but his friend Asselineau noticed that Gérard had no overcoat. It was apparently in the pawnshop, for Nerval needed money. He talked of *Aurélia,* the first part of which had just appeared in the *Revue de Paris.* On the 24th of January he wrote his last letter to his aunt:

Good, dear aunt, —tell your son he doesn't know that you are the best of mothers and of aunts. When I have triumphed completely, you will have your place in my Olympus, for I have my place in your home. Do not expect me this evening, for the night will be black and white. [*Ne m'attends pas ce soir, car la nuit sera noire et blanche.*]

Gérard showed his friends what was perhaps an apron-string; but he identified it as the girdle that Mme de Maintenon had worn at St. Cyr when her girls had put on Racine's *Esther*. Others have said he called it the garter of Marguerite de Valois or of the Duchesse de Longueville or of the Queen of Sheba.

The eve of January 26 Gérard put on what clothes he had left, including a top hat and gray cloth gaiters, and set out into the bitter cold of the Parisian winter night. In a dingy alley-way known as the Street of the Old Lantern (la Rue de la Vieille Lanterne), he apparently knocked very late at the door of a wretched hovel to find a sleeping place. If so, no one seems to have answered. At dawn they found Gérard hanging from the bar of a window by his apron-string that had been for him the garter of the Queen of Sheba or of Marguerite de Valois or of the Duchesse de Longueville, or the girdle that Mme de Maintenon had worn at St. Cyr.

The present Sarah Bernhardt Theatre stands on the location of the Rue de la Vieille Lanterne where Gérard came that winter night so long ago with his gaiters buckled on for the other world. There is a peculiar irony in the detail furnished by the *Figaro Littéraire* of January 15, 1955 that at that date the precise site of Gérard's death a century before was occupied by the prompter's box of the theatre, for some have thought that Gérard's suicide was motivated, at least in part, by his failure as a dramatist.

We cannot know about this. But it is clear that what lay behind the dream gates, of which he had written so beautifully in his last work, could not finally suffice for Gérard in life. One can still hear over the years, as a sort of valediction, the last words he wrote to "the best of mothers and of aunts":

Ne m'attends pas ce soir, car la nuit sera noire et blanche.
[Do not expect me this evening, for the night will be black and white.]

Did he mean a night pitch-black and sleepless (*une nuit blanche* in French is a sleepless night)? Or was it rather dark night to be followed by white dawn — in Dom Pernety's terms the alchemical "Resurrection," the passing from the black of death to white in the operation of the Great Work? Or was it for Gérard merely a reference to the death he sought that last night in the darkness and the snow? However it may be, in that bitter winter dawn, in the Street of the Old Lantern, for Gérard de Nerval the dream gates closed forever in this world.

IV

A REBOURS, HUYSMANS AND THE DECADENT WAY

IT IS NOW many years since I first read *The Picture of Dorian Gray* and came upon Wilde's famous passage that is supposed to refer to *A rebours (Against the Grain).* I had read nothing of Huysmans at the time and wondered at the peculiar nature of the book that Wilde described. It was supposed to have "poisoned" Dorian Gray, and Wilde's description still affords an interesting passage from the period of the Yellow Nineties in England:

> [Dorian's] eye fell on the yellow book that Lord Henry had sent him. What was it, he wondered. He ... flung himself into an armchair and began to turn over the leaves. After a few minutes he became absorbed. It was the strangest book that he had ever read. It seemed to him that in exquisite raiment, and to the delicate sound of flutes, the sins of the world were passing in dumb show before him. Things that he had dimly dreamed of were suddenly made real to him. Things of which he had never dreamed were gradually revealed.
>
> It was a novel without a plot, and with only one character, being, indeed, simply a psychological study of a certain young Parisian, who spent his life trying to realize in the nineteenth century all the passions and modes of thought that belonged to every century except his own, and to sum up, as it were, in himself the various moods through which the world-spirit had ever passed. ... The life of the senses was described in the terms of mystical philosophy. One hardly knew at times whether one was reading the ecstasies of some mediaeval saint or the morbid confessions of a modern sinner. It was a poisonous book. The heavy odour of incense seemed to cling about its

pages and to trouble the brain. The mere cadence of the sentences, the subtle monotony of their music, so full as it was of complex refrains and movements elaborately repeated, produced in the mind of the lad, as he passed from chapter to chapter, a form of reverie, a malady of dreaming, that made him unconscious of the falling day and creeping shadows. . . .

For years, Dorian Gray could not free himself from the influence of this book.

As we shall see hereafter, this is not a very accurate description of *Against the Grain,* though it has its own special pertinence to the novel, from which it clearly derived certain of its details, and it helped to arouse an odd kind of interest in Huysmans outside of France. After all, who could fail to be curious about the "poison" in the strangest book that Dorian Gray had ever read? It is with this book, its author, and its significance in relation to the decadent and another way that we shall be primarily concerned this evening.

*   *   *

In the title of my lecture, "*A rebours,* Huysmans and the Decadent Way," the word *decadent* poses at once a question of pronunciation. I prefer *decádent* with its emphasis on the sense of decay, though the meaning of the word is not of necessity entirely pejorative. Others will prefer *décadent,* which has a sort of phonetic symbolism in its weak sound, as if something in the word itself were about to give way.

As for meaning, I shall not try to be quite so definite and shall allow the sense to emerge more or less from the context; but we may turn for a hint first of all to the Latin etymology *de* + *cadere* "to fall down (*or* away) from," in the sense especially of falling away from an earlier quality or standard of excellence. *The Oxford Dictionary of English Etymology* (1966) gives the adjective *decadent,* derived from the French, as being used specifically in 1884 by Maurice Barrès "to designate a French literary movement"; and we may note that 1884 is precisely the publication year of Huysmans' *A rebours.*

Now, falling away from an earlier standard may not necessarily be a disaster. It may even entail desirable new developments and the emergence of new values and qualities. Moreover, a significant writer in a decadent period need not be essentially a decadent writer, as John Middleton Murry insisted many years ago in an essay on Baudelaire. With *A rebours,* as we shall see, decadent elements seem to predominate, although there are ambiguities throughout the novel and in the hero's character that raise problems of interpretation, and the ultimate influence of the book has been quite different from what one would expect.

As early as 1834 Désiré Nisard had developed at some length parallels between French literature of the nineteenth century and the literature of the Latin decadence; but the most arresting and influential passages suggesting such parallels occur in a note appended by Baudelaire to his poem "Franciscae meae laudes" of 1857, and in Théophile Gautier's expansion of its ideas in his *notice* ("Charles Baudelaire") for the 1868 edition of *Les Fleurs du Mal* which was perhaps the most influential essay ever written on the subject of decadent style.

According to Gautier . . .

> . . . what is improperly called the style of decadence . . . is really only art arrived at the point of extreme maturity determined by the oblique suns of civilizations that are growing old: a style ingenious, complicated, learned, full of nuances and carefully sought out effects, forever thrusting back the limits of the language, borrowing from all the technical vocabularies, taking its colors from all palettes, its notes from all keyboards, striving to express what is most ineffable in thought, what is most vague and fleeting in the contours of form. . . . This style of decadence is the last word of the Verb called upon for total expression and driven to its ultimate extremity. One can recall, on the subject, the language of the late Roman empire already veined like marble with the greens of decomposition and as it were gamy with age and the complicated refinements of the Byzantine school, the final form of Greek art that had fallen to deliquescence; but such is indeed the necessary and predestined idiom of peoples and civilizations in which artificial life has replaced natural life and developed needs that were formerly unknown.

And Gautier cites Baudelaire's note to "Franciscae meae laudes," which, he says, "explains and corroborates what we have just said about the idioms of decadence." We shall soon see much of all this mirrored in the *A rebours* of Joris-Karl Huysmans and in the mind of its decadent hero.

The idea of French decadence was in the air during these years, and it flourished especially for several decades after the defeat and humiliations of the Franco-Prussian War of 1870. It became fashionable, even, during these years to see France as occupying the position of the decaying Roman Empire at the time of the last barbarian invasions; and the parallel was naturally drawn also between the barbarians of those ancient days and the contemporary invading Germans. We find such ideas, for example, in the review called *Le Chat Noir* in 1883 (the year before the publication of *A rebours*) in a sonnet by Verlaine ("Langueur") that is said to have become a sort of *art poétique* for the decadents of the day:

> Je suis l'Empire à la fin de la décadence,
> Qui regarde passer les grands Barbares blancs. . . .
>
> [I am the Empire at the end of its decline,
> Watching the tall blond Barbarians go by. . . .]

By the 1890s the idea of French decadence was a commonplace in certain circles, and violent critics like Max Nordau and Dr. Emile Laurent exploited it with notable exuberance. Nordau, in a long, vitriolic, two-volume work called *Entartung* (*Degeneration* [1892-93]), said some very unpleasant things about Huysmans and his hero (whom he called "a parasite of the lowest grade of atavism, a sort of human sacculus" — with a vivid footnote clarification of the term), and he found in common among the French Symbolists "all the signs of degeneracy and imbecility." In a preface to the work dedicated to Lombroso, Nordau even observed that "degenerates are not always criminals, prostitutes, anarchists, and pronounced lunatics; they are often authors and artists."

Dr. Laurent proclaimed equally remarkable discoveries in his book on *La poésie décadente devant la science psychiatrique* (1897), in which he identified such physical traits as a lack of forehead, prognathous features, deformed noses, wide ears, and oddly shaped heads as characteristic of a "decadent physiognomy"; and he claimed to discover such traits in French decadent poets of the day. Two years earlier George Bernard Shaw had published an essay against Nordau on "The Sanity of Art," in which he refuted such nonsense. But Dr. Laurent had probably not read it.

All in all, there was notable controversy in Europe over such matters in the arts, and Huysmans had played a significant role in bringing it about. One can see him even almost in the role of *provocateur* when one considers some of the outlandish experiments and opinions he devises for his decadent hero in *A rebours*.

*   *   *

Huysmans tells us that the ancestors of the Floressas des Esseintes, so far as one can tell from their portraits, were a fierce and warlike race — but that their descendants in later ages wore themselves out in dissipation and intermarriage until only one was left in the direct line, le duc Jean des Esseintes, an anaemic and nervous young aesthete of thirty. His mother had died of exhaustion and his father of some vague illness when des Esseintes was seventeen. His childhood had been gloomy, except for his study with the Jesuits, under whose guidance he had learned Latin with delight, but was a dullard in Greek, modern tongues and the sciences. At home he grew up, largely neglected by his parents, in a world of old, bored servants, reading and dreaming, and returned to school after vacations with a world of his own in his head. His teachers ultimately let him go his own way, recognizing his restless and roving intelligence. When he attains his majority and comes into his inheritance, he leaves his Jesuit teachers behind. He finds his surviving relatives old and mummy-like and his contemporaries empty and dull — even the men of letters among them banal and uninteresting. He comes to scorn humanity and sees the world as inhabited mostly by imbeciles, and he begins to dream of some place of refuge where he can live apart from what he considers "the unending deluge of human stupidity." He has grown weary of dissipation, suffers from immense boredom, and is a victim of nervous disorders. Finally, the medical diagnoses of his doctors and recognition of his depleted fortune frighten him into changing his extravagant and debilitating way of life. He settles his affairs and finds a modest dwelling in Fontenay-aux-Roses, a remote suburb of Paris where he can be alone. Then, when the new property has been arranged to his taste, he gets rid of his furniture and his servants and disappears without leaving so much as an address behind. And thus begin the ultimate decadent adventures of le duc des Esseintes — one of the strangest figures in the fiction of the nineteenth century.

Various models have been suggested for Huysmans' decadent duke, and one can see certain elements of his habits and character in such earlier figures as Passereau l'Ecolier in Petrus Borel's *Contes immoraux,* C. Auguste Dupin and Roderick Usher in the tales of Poe, and Samuel Cramer, the hero of Baudelaire's prose narrative called *La Fanfarlo.* There are also Francis Poictevin and the hero of the Goncourt brothers' novel *Charles Demailly.* And finally there is Count Robert de Montesquiou-Fezensac, a Parisian aesthete who had a gilded turtle and immense social prestige and fancied himself a poet by virtue of having published such volumes of verse as *Les chauves souris (The Bats)* and *Les hortensias bleus (The Blue Hydrangias).* Montesquiou has been further identified as one of the models for Proust's Baron de Charlus in *A la recherche du temps perdu.* But he was never quite so consistently and impressively decadent as le duc des Esseintes.

Huysmans' hero sets about putting in order his new quarters in the house at Fontenay. He decides that his earlier eccentricities and affectations were puerile and rearranges the organization of his life. First there is the matter of colors, for des Esseintes begins with the visual sense in his experiments with sensation. Since he hardly comes alive except at night, particular nuances of colors must be arranged for effects in artificially lighted rooms. One after another various colors and shades are considered and discarded until only red, orange and yellow remain. Des Esseintes chooses orange, and his reasons afford an instructive index to his thought.

It seems to des Esseintes that, among those whose eyes are refined by literature and art, the idealists prefer blue and its derivatives such as mauve, lilac and pearl-gray — the plethoric males, on the other hand, choose the brilliant lights of yellows and reds that blind and intoxicate the senses — but, finally, the eyes of weak and irritable spirits with sensual appetites that desire highly seasoned dishes usually take delight in "that irritating and unhealthy color, with its artificial splendors, its acid fevers: orange." So des Esseintes examines all the effects of this color under artificial lights and finally has his study walls bound like books in an orange hue of crushed morocco leather, and has the plinths and moldings painted dark indigo.

The only luxuries here were to be his books and rare flowers, but des Esseintes does have a massive fifteenth-century table and an old wrought-iron lectern, which has on it a ponderous folio volume of Du Cange's *Glossarium mediae et infimae latinitatis*. The bluish window-panes let in a dim light upon the dark gold of the curtains. In this room are displayed three compositions of Baudelaire copied on vellum with splendid illuminations: a sonnet from *Les Fleurs du Mal* on each side ("The Death of the Lovers" and "The Enemy") and in the middle the prose poem entitled (in English) "Anywhere Out of the World."

In his new home des Esseintes has no one but two old servants, and he arranges their schedules so that they are seldom seen or heard. His active hours are at odds with those of normal life. In winter he has a light breakfast at five in the afternoon as darkness comes on, takes dinner about an hour before midnight, and has another light repast about five in the morning before retiring.

His private dining-room is arranged to resemble a ship's cabin and is inserted, like a Japanese box, inside a larger room. Here there is a spacious aquarium whose waters, artificially colored to his taste of the moment, are occupied by artificial fish that are all wound up like clocks. Various maritime instruments lie about here and there, and a smell of tar is blown into the room to give des Esseintes a further illusion of being aboard ship. There is a single book on the table — Poe's *Adventures of Arthur Gordon Pym,* bound in sealskin and privately printed on laid paper with a sea-gull watermark.

Thus des Esseintes lives in his imagination. It is his opinion that nature has had her day and that artifice is the hall-mark of human genius. He seeks refuge here from the insentience and bad manners that had so infuriated him in the Paris he had known.

Des Esseintes' library reminds one vaguely of Roderick Usher's; but it is described in far greater detail and covers many more authors, although it is still peculiarly limited to its creator's decadent tastes.

A portion of the shelves on the orange and indigo walls of des Esseintes' study is devoted entirely to Latin works of the so-called "decadence." Des Esseintes has no taste for the Latin language of

the Age of Augustus, finding its syntax rigid and the language itself
colorless, smoothed down until it has lost its vitality — a language
repetitious and full of commonplaces. In fact, no later linguistic
period bored him so much again until he came to the age of French
Classicism under Louis XIV. It was thus only with Lucan's
Pharsalia that des Esseintes began to be interested in the Latin
tongue.

Here we see already something of Huysmans' characteristic
tone in *A rebours*. The appreciations of decadent Latin writing are
so engagingly presented that one may not at first be wholly conscious of their monstrous eccentricity. Des Esseintes seems, for
example, hardly to have considered the Greeks, and he summarily
dismisses, with derisive criticism, all the major Latin writers cited
from the Augustan Age, only to express his special delight in the
Satyricon of Petronius and his pleasure in Apuleius and in such
poets of the fourth and fifth centuries of the Christian era as
Claudian, Rutilius and Ausonius. He neglects St. Jerome and
St. Augustine for Prudentius, Apollonius Sidonius and Marius
Victorinus. He enjoys Fortunatus, bishop of Poitiers, for hymns like
the *Vexilla regis,* which he finds "carved from the old carrion of the
Latin tongue and made pungent by the aromatic spices of
the Church"; and he finds to his taste Boethius, Gregory of Tours,
Paul the Deacon, and Walafrid Strabo — the last especially for his
Hortulus with its chapters glorifying the pumpkin as the symbol
of fecundity.

Except for a scattering of miscellaneous volumes on the Cabala,
medicine, botany, patrology, erotology and the like, des Esseintes'
Latin books end with the tenth century. Then, "in a formidable
leap . . . the books aligned next on the shelves, skipping the transi-
tion of the ages, went directly to the French language of the
nineteenth century."

Much of all this seems to reflect Huysmans' own thought and
taste. But there is something in the tone and in the nature of
numerous details that suggests the wisdom of keeping one's tongue
in cheek as he reads; and this impression is enhanced when one
comes upon the ensuing interrelated episodes of the turtle, the
dentist, and the mouth-organ.

Late one afternoon when des Esseintes is having breakfast a
lapidary arrives with a great, resplendent, live turtle in his arms.

This resulted from a whim of des Esseintes, who had decided one day that his Oriental rug needed some moving contrast to bring out its colors. He had brought in the turtle first in its own native hues, but saw at once that its dull carapace would not accomplish what he sought. Next he had it gilded; but the brilliant glow of the gold still left him unsatisfied. He decided finally that upon the golden shell there should be mounted a delicate pattern wrought in precious stones, and he set about arranging a Japanese floral design and selecting with great and erudite care the jewels that were to go into its composition. The rather bemused lapidary had taken down all the directions and had faithfully carried them out. So now at last des Esseintes has his turtle adorned to his taste, glowing in the subdued light of his dining-room. He feels very happy as he looks at it and even, for once, develops a slight appetite for his delicate meal and dips his toast into his impeccable brew of yellow Chinese tea with more than usual relish. Then he reenters his study and has his servant bring him the turtle, which has remained persistently motionless.

Snow is falling outside, and des Esseintes' room is very still in the shadows. The hearth-logs glow as he remains lost in revery. He opens a window, sees the dark sky overhead and feels a chilling wind. Then comes a passage that takes one back to the theories of the Abbé Polycarpe Poncelet in the eighteenth century and marks a continuation of des Esseinte's earlier experiments with the senses — but with a shift from visual to gustatory sensation.

> ... [Des Esseintes] drew himself close to the fire and had the idea of taking a draught of spirits to warm himself.
>
> He entered the dining room where, built into one of the partitions, there was a cupboard that held a series of little barrels, lined up side by side, on very small frames of sandalwood, pierced at the bottom by little silver spigots.
>
> He called this collection of liquor-casks his mouth-organ.
>
> A small rod was so arranged that it could link all the spigots and control them with a single movement so that, once the apparatus was in place, it sufficed to touch a button hidden in the woodwork to open all the little taps

at the same time and fill with liquor the tiny cups arranged beneath them.

The organ was now open. The stops labelled "flute," "horn," "voix céleste" were drawn out, ready to play. Des Esseintes sipped a drop here, another there, playing himself inner symphonies, and managed to attain in his throat sensations analogous to those that music affords for the ear.

Moreover, the taste of each liquor corresponded in his opinion to the sound of a particular musical instrument. Dry curaçao, for example, was like the clarinet, whose tone is tart and velvety; kümmel was like the oboe, whose sonorous timbre has a nasal twang; crême de menthe and anisette resembled the flute, at once sugary and pungent, whining and sweet; then, to complete the orchestra, kirsch gives the furious sound of the trumpet, gin and whiskey blast the palate with their strident notes of cornets and trombones, liqueur brandy roars with the deafening crash of tubas, while the thunders of the cymbals and the bass drum beaten with full force roll in the mouth by means of the *rakis de Chio* and the mastics!

Des Esseintes goes further to play string quartets on his palate, with old brandy for the violin, rum for the alto, vespetro for the violoncello and fine old bitter beer for the double-bass, "full-bodied, solid and black." He finds that the minor key of Benedictine corresponds to the major key of alcohols in green Chartreuse. He even manages to transfer to his palate the scores of real musical compositions. "But tonight, des Esseintes ... confined himself to sounding one single note on the keyboard of his instrument, by filling a tiny cup with genuine Irish whisky. ..."

He finds in the drink a strong taste of creosote, and this taste takes him suddenly back to an earlier experience. He recalls a horrible visit to a ferocious dentist for a tooth extraction. The fellow had got his forceps on the tooth and begun to pull, and the terrified aesthete had stamped his feet in agony, seen stars, and bleated like a sheep being slaughtered. His tooth had broken off, and he had howled and fought until the dentist had finally come up with the rest of the shell and the root. Spitting blood, des Esseintes had emerged into the street below feeling suddenly alive again and ten years younger. Yet even now he shuddered at the memory of that awful experience, and to get it out of his mind he arose and went to look for his turtle.

It still had not moved. He felt it and found that it was dead.

*   *   *

Huysmans furnishes a remarkable description of des Esseintes' paintings and engravings, among which his favorites are such works as Gustave Moreau's *Salomé* and *The Apparition,* depicting scenes concerned with the decapitation of John the Baptist — Bresdin's *Comedy of Death* — the drawings of Odilon Redon that seem to des Esseintes to be products of illness and delirium — a sinister El Greco — and a lugubrious series of engravings of *Religious Persecutions* by the Dutch Calvinist Jan Luyken. As he examines his collection des Esseintes finds Paris very far away and imagines himself deep in a cloister far from the secular world.

One day (in what Huysmans later referred to as "the terrible Chapter VI") des Esseintes recalls two very unsavory and cynical experiments he has attempted in human engineering — the first in helping arrange a marriage for a friend when he knew it would end in misery for both partners, and the second an apparently unsuccessful attempt to lead a young boy into a life of crime. In this second venture, after all his plans were carefully laid, des Esseintes had settled back and watched the newspapers for the results of his handiwork, expecting to read of the boy's arrest for robbery or murder. But he looked in vain and finally gave up in disgust. "The little Judas!" he murmurs in irritation. Then, noting that it is 3:00 in the morning, he lights a cigarette and goes back to the book he was reading before his revery — "the old Latin poem *De laude castitatis,* written in the reign of Godebald, by Avitus, the metropolitan bishop of Vienne."

As the days pass des Esseintes gives in to vague musings, and his mind turns to religious speculations until he begins to fear that a breach is developing in his scepticism. He realizes that much of his strange quest is rooted in his years with the Jesuits, and he finds himself more influenced by them than he had thought. He comes almost to fear a sudden religious conversion and thinks he is becoming stupid. His mind whirls in thoughts of religious processions, great cathedrals, sacrilege and the Devil, the Satanic Mass and the Witches Sabbath, and he has a panoramic vision of the Church over the ages. He turns for relief to the "salutary pessimism" of Schopenhauer; but his nervous disorders return, and he finally gives up even reading and decides to embark upon an experiment in exquisitely perverse horticulture.

Des Esseintes had always been passionately fond of flowers, but had long since lost all pleasure in the ordinary varieties. His floral tastes had developed in the same directions as his tastes in art and literature. In the old days in Paris he had once arranged a marvellous collection of artificial flowers, made by gifted artists to imitate real flowers in all their various conditions from bud to withered bloom, covered with dewdrops, or with falling leaves. This had amused him for a while; but now a different whim stirred his imagination: to substitute for artificial flowers that looked real, real flowers that would appear artificial. To this end he wore himself out in expeditions to greenhouses and spent large sums on bizarre plants, marvelling at the floral monstrosities he had come upon. When they are all assembled, des Esseintes can hardly contain his enthusiasm. The collection has the appearance of some monstrous hospital exhibit. It seems a splendid proof of man's ability at last to shape nature to his desires. Des Esseintes decides that the only true artists are horticulturists and, a little weary of all his exertion and excitement, goes to lie down on his bed, where he has a hideous nightmare inspired by his monstrous flowers.

When nightmares continue and he feels pains in his legs, temples and jaws and suffers from increasing insomnia and nervous disorders he loses interest in his plants, most of which are now dying, and feels unutterably bored. Finally, he turns to Dickens' novels; but the chaste English heroines and the whiff of English cant that rises from the pages have an ironically perverse effect and recall his various love affairs (what Huysmans calls with an Augustinian loathing "ses vieux cloaques"). None of these relationships had lasted long or left any deep feeling when it ended. A violet bonbon on des Esseintes' tongue recalls various figures clearly to his memory: Miss Urania, an American circus acrobat whose masculine appearance charmed him, but who was ultimately a great disappointment — and a trail of others, vulgar and perverse, including a little, dark-haired ventriloquist whose art brought to life in his room the dialogue between the Sphinx and the Chimaera from Flaubert's *Temptation of Saint Anthony*.

Then one day des Esseintes begins to suffer from olfactory hallucinations. He seems to smell constantly the repugnant scent of red jasmine or frangipane and resolves to get rid of it by experimenting with real perfumes. Here Huysmans describes his hero's adventures with a third of the senses; and the details of the experiment are as exaggerated as those in the famous episode of the "mouth-organ."

In his dressing-room des Esseintes approaches an array of essence-bottles of all forms and sizes and divides them into two series: simple extracts and perfume compounds or *bouquets*. He had long believed that the sense of smell could give pleasures equal to those of seeing and hearing — that, in fact, a trained nose could distinguish the *bouquet* of a true artist from the pot-pourri made by someone for the trade just as surely as a trained ear could distinguish a composition by Beethoven from one by Clapisson. The artist shapes the fragrance to the original natural odor and sets it off, much as a jeweler sets off the limpidity and lustre of a gem. Des Esseintes had studied the secrets of the perfumer's art — working at what he considered the grammar and syntax of odors until he could analyse the style of the great *parfumeurs* and trace their art in France through its classical and romantic periods, as it followed the path of the French language itself — from Saint-Amant and Bossuet to Hugo and Gautier and the influences of China and Japan.

Des Esseintes had collected all sorts of rare balms and essences, and he dreams of concocting a new *bouquet* like a writer beginning a new work. He experiments a little before getting under way, arranging various combinations, becoming more and more sure of himself, and determined to get rid of the persistent "whisper" of frangipane. He builds his perfume on an analogy with poems of Baudelaire and is distracted by dreams evoked through the "aromatic stanzas" in the "fragrant orchestration" of his poem. He injects various essences into the room with vaporizers and mingles these with other mixtures.

A ventilator prepares the way for new combinations. Des Esseintes arranges odors that suggest an immense countryside with scents of lilacs and lime trees, then the presence of women, then a deserted region, then factories with smoking chimneys, then a region fragrant with new-mown hay, and finally a mélange of landscapes and odors amidst which, like a refrain, there recurs the odor of the great meadow with the fragrance of lilacs and lime trees.

A sharp pain cuts through his head, and des Esseintes puts the stoppers back in his bottles and opens the window over the valley of Fontenay. Various odors come to him standing there until finally the scent of frangipane recurs so powerfully that he falls in a faint, all but dying, at his open window.

The doctor, who is hastily called by the servants, can make nothing of his patient's disorder and leaves quite overcome by the eccentric furnishings of the dwelling he has entered. In a few days des Esseintes recovers by himself from his seizure and decides finally to take a long trip to relieve his boredom — an adventure whose narration affords one of the high spots in Huysmans' novel of a decadent life.

The wretched weather — misty, then gray with fine rain — puts des Esseintes in mind of London and, still under the influence of Dickens, he is tempted to visit the great metropolis across the Channel. After careful preparation he sets out finally, with his old servant staggering under the weight of a trunk, a valise, a night bag, a hat-box, and an assortment of canes and umbrellas. The train to Paris goes under dark skies and upon arrival in the French capital des Esseintes takes a cab to *Galignani's Messenger* in the Rue de Rivoli to purchase a Baedeker. When he comes out, the wind whips the rain against the arcades, and he drives to an English place called the "Bodega" for a drink. He orders a glass of port. All about him are English surroundings and Americans and Englishmen — clergymen dressed in black, and bulldog-faced men with apoplectic necks, ears like tomatoes, and the eyes of idiots. Watching the flow of dark red port, des Esseintes imagines that all those around him are characters out of Dickens. He imagines also domestic scenes with Little Dorrit and Dora Copperfield. The tugboats behind the Tuileries seem to him to be coming along the Thames. He finishes his port and calls for a glass of Amontillado, and at sight of the pale dry wine he recalls Poe's nightmare story and discovers sinister expressions on the commonplace faces around him. He is startled to find that it is already time for dinner, pays for his drinks and leaves.

The rain comes in gusts and obscures the light from the street-lamps. Des Esseintes calls his cabby and sets out for an English tavern on the Rue d'Amsterdam near the railroad station. He has just time to dine before catching the boat train. He should be in London at 12:30 the next afternoon.

Surrounded now by English men and English women with wide teeth which clamp down resolutely on rumpsteak pie, des Esseintes feels hungrier than he has felt in a long while. He orders ox-tail soup, a haddock, roast beef with potatoes and two pints of ale, nibbles at a bit of blue Stilton cheese, at a rhubarb tart, and has a glass of porter. He has not eaten so much in years. He sits back in his chair, lights a cigarette and sips his coffee laced with gin. He hears the rain against the window-panes outside, watches the Englishmen getting up — all dressed alike — and feels himself a sort of naturalized citizen of London. He has a half hour still before train time.

He recalls a disillusioning trip he had once taken to Holland, led astray at the Louvre by the Dutch painters who had served as a springboard for his dreams. In spite of his enjoyment of Haarlem and Amsterdam, he had found Holland on the whole not at all what he had expected, and he recalls his disenchantment as he sees by his watch that he has only ten minutes left to catch his train. He drinks a glass of brandy as a stirrup-cup and calls for his check.

Then a languor passes through him. "Why budge," he asks himself, "when one can travel so magnificently in his chair?" After all, he has really been in London with all this English atmosphere and all these Englishmen around him. Why risk another disappointment? He would have to run for it now to catch his train. Why risk losing the wonderful English impressions he has stored up during the past few hours?

He looks at his watch again. It is time to go home. And des Esseintes orders the cabby to take him back to the Sceaux station and returns to Fontenay with his trunk, his valise, his night bag, his hat-box and his assortment of canes and umbrellas. He arrives in a state of physical and moral exhaustion like a man home at last after a long and dangerous journey.

*   *   *

After his return from London des Esseintes reorganizes his library on the shelves and examines his modern books. Before the nineteenth century he cares for very few French writings aside from Villon's *ballades,* bits of d'Aubigné, the preachers Bourdaloue and Bossuet, and the *pensées* of Nicole and Pascal. He thus neglects most of the major authors in French literature before his own century, just as he had overlooked the Greeks completely and avoided the Latin writers of the Age of Augustus in forming the earlier part of his library.

In the contemporary period his favorite authors are Baudelaire and, especially, Poe, whom he finds "deep and strange." It is Poe who answers best to his needs — most of all in his analyses of the will in the regions of morbid psychology as it is influenced by lethargy or terror. Des Esseintes is fascinated by Poe's "Imp of the Perverse" (which today, like *The Black Cat,* seems to have anticipated some elements of the *acte gratuit,* so famous in later literature). He is attracted also to Poe's neurotic and mysterious heroines (his Morellas and Ligeias), and he feels on occasion a peculiar kinship with the morbid hero of *The Fall of the House of Usher.*

Among Catholic writers, des Esseintes prefers Barbey d'Aurevilly for his works hovering between mysticism and sadism. His favorite literary form is the prose poem, among whose masterpieces he identifies Mallarmé's "Plainte d'automne" and "Frisson d'hiver." As for the poets, aside from his favorite Baudelaire he prefers Verlaine and Corbière and Mallarmé.

In these pages many of Huysmans' appreciations are still of interest, and they helped to introduce little-known authors to the literate public. It is worth noting here that des Esseintes preferred Flaubert's *Temptation of Saint Anthony* and *Salammbô* to his *Sentimental Education* (*Madame Bovary* is not even mentioned), the Goncourts' *Faustin* to their *Germinie Lacerteux,* and Zola's *The Sin of Abbé Mouret* to his *L'Assommoir.* Des Esseintes was especially attracted to *Faustin* for its morbid, impressionistic style which he considered comparable to the Latin styles of Ausonius, Claudian and Rutilius.

But for des Esseintes it was in Mallarmé above all that decadent literature seemed to have come to its end. He smiled as he looked at his folio volume open on the chapel lectern, and it occurred to him that some day a scholar would prepare a great dictionary of the decadence of the French language like the one that Du Cange had made for the old Latin as it sounded its death-rattle from the depths of the mediaeval cloisters.

A period of oppressively hot weather arouses in des Esseintes all sorts of neurotic symptoms. He longs for what he considers his former healthy days when, in the full heat of summer, he found some relief by wrapping himself in furs and climbing into a sleigh. Then, with his teeth chattering, he had remarked how cold the wind was and how he was freezing until he almost convinced himself that the day was bitterly cold. In those times, too, he used to arouse visions by taking opium and hashish; but now the drugs merely upset his stomach and bring on a fearful attack of nerves.

Des Esseintes suffers once more from nightmares and from olfactory and auditory hallucinations. The latter recall his old pleasure in the plain-chant, in which he identified the true soul of the middle ages, the everlasting hymn rising to God over all the years. He remembers the magnificant sound of the "De profundis" and thinks how affected even the finest other music sounds beside its austere majesty.

One morning, after seeing his face in the mirror staring out at him like a death's head, des Esseintes in terror calls the doctor, who prescribes a peptone enema as the beginning of his cure. It occurs to des Esseintes when the remedy appears to be salutary that this procedure is, in a way, a crowning achievement for a life of artifice. If only the routine could be adopted permanently! What a protest against the deadly sin of gluttony! — and, best of all, what a triumph over nature! But his doctor upsets all his dream by getting him up and about and then insisting that he must return to Paris and lead a more normal existence. It is a matter of life or death, and the doctor poses a rather startling alternative: either follow a more normal routine and be healthy, or persist in his present way of life and suffer from madness complicated by tuberculosis. "Then it is either death or the hulks!" says des Esseintes in his exasperation. But the doctor merely smiles and leaves without another word. And des Esseintes has to make up his mind.

As one thinks back over the details and episodes in the decadent life that Huysmans has described in *A rebours* one is likely to find them, beyond their artifice and brilliant exaggeration, in some unexpected way, suddenly sad and empty. It is as if the fun had gone out of things. Perhaps there is a pathos in all des Esseintes' subtle thought and organization behind each episode — or in the peculiar sense of urgency that Huysmans manages to keep alive amidst the fatuous details — or in the fact that (except for des Esseintes' artistic and literary enthusiasms) there is no sense of human affection or understanding anywhere in this strange and lonely life.

The incidents, seen in retrospect in terms of des Esseintes' final despair, appear less as ridiculous affectations than as hopeless ventures along a series of connected paths that always terminate in a blind alley. It is like a multiplication of Emma Bovary's dark corridor with its fast-shut door. As one looks back upon them (the study bound in orange-hued morocco leather with dark indigo moldings, whose carefully sought colors finally lost their charm — the aquarium with its mechanical fish — the decadent library — the gilded and bejewelled turtle that dies — the mouth-organ — the morbid paintings and engravings — the attempt to lead a young boy to crime — the experiment in monstrous horticulture that ends with a mass of hideous dead plants — the love relationships without any human affection, culminating in the short-lived affair with a female ventriloquist — the experiment with the syntax of perfumes that leads to a nervous collapse — the absurd London journey — memories of the summer fantasy in the sleigh as representative of a healthy period in des Esseintes' life — and, finally, the peptone enema that seems for a brief while so desirable and magnificent a triumph over gluttony and nature) the whole progress of these disillusioning experiments and imaginings is seen coming to an end when the doctor gives his peculiar diagnosis and orders his patient's return to a more normal life. It is perhaps worth recalling that it was des Esseintes' sight of his own face like a death's head in the mirror that made him call for help.

The acuteness of des Esseintes' despair is brought home in the closing passage of *A rebours* as he prepares to return to Paris. The terminus of his decadent way is a dead end, like all its separate corridors. But, if des Esseintes despairs of this, he sees no hope for an exit any other way. The philosophy of pessimism is no longer of any help, and he realizes at last that the only solace for him would be what he considers impossible — belief in a future life. He watches clean-shaven men and his old servant carrying out his belongings from the house in Fontenay. In misery he falls into a chair and the book ends in his cry of lonely anguish:

> ... In two days, I shall be in Paris; ah, well ... it is all over; like a flow of the tide, the waves of human mediocrity rise up to the sky and will engulf the refuge whose dikes I unwillingly open. Ah! courage fails me and my heart breaks! —Lord, take pity on the Christian who doubts, on the unbeliever who would believe, on the convict of life setting out alone, in the night, under a sky no longer lighted by the consoling beacons of the ancient hope!

* * *

Des Esseintes' pursuit of the imagination and the sensations for their own sake is closely related to the ideal of "l'Art pour l'Art" and marks an aspect of man's stress on the immediate, material present for his values, without lasting concern for past or future. Moreover, *A rebours* seems to me a culminating point in the modern literature of decadence. After such a book the arrival of a demolition movement like Dadaism seems inescapable — and thereafter, in a continuing, logical development, such resultant movements as Surrealism and the atheistic Existentialism of Jean-Paul Sartre. Here the motion has been, in turn, from a despairing falling away from established values in an appeal to immediate sensations *(A rebours)* — to a temporary nihilism (in Dada) — to a call upon the undisciplined subliminal individual consciousness (in Surrealism) — and, when that wore thin, to acceptance of an austere moral responsibility for choice in a world of values limited to a nontranscendent view of man (in Sartre's Existentialism). As we have seen in our own day, the ultimate, key word in this direction of man's thought has been *absurdity*.

There is no question but that the quest of des Esseintes came to a dead end. The cry of frustration and lonely anguish at the last suggests no way out in its own terms from the decadent way.

But there is an irony finally in the ensuing history and influence of Huysmans' *A rebours* — and it is perhaps what one might have expected from a certain ambiguity of tone that persists in this most famous narrative of decadence. *A rebours* is never quite a parody or a caricature; but one has a continuing sense of there being in it a tongue-in-cheek quality, as if Huysmans himself sensed other more important forces in motion behind the scenes.

Des Esseintes is a character of fiction; but he prefigures certain significant qualities in his creator, and Huysmans was a living man. His "Preface Written Twenty Years after the Novel" may help us to understand some of the puzzling aspects of his book.

Huysmans tells us that Naturalism was at its height when he wrote *A rebours* and that he himself (an early follower of the movement) was trying vaguely without any clear plan, to escape from a *cul-de-sac* in which he was suffocating. In writing *A rebours* he found himself doing careful research for each chapter on various aspects of different arts — for example, on gem stones, perfumes, flowers, religious and secular literature, profane music, and plain-chant. As he worked he began gradually to see that mediaeval art existed only in and through the Church, and he tells us that he began to wonder "how a religion that seemed to be made for children had been able to suggest such marvellous works."

He prowled around the Church, as it were, without thinking himself close to religion. "It did not occur to me," he writes, "that from Schopenhauer whom I admired irrationally, it is only a step to Ecclesiastes and the Book of Job." As he looks back at *A rebours* he sees now that it contained in germ all his later writings. There were hints in it that prepared one for his next book, *Là-bas (Down There),* a study of Gilles de Rais and the Black Mass which has been called "the most important novel on Satanism in any language." Huysmans tells us that in *En route* and *L'Oblat,* there-after, he examined the mediaeval Latin more profoundly in treating the liturgy. In *La Cathédrale* he developed further the superficial chapter in *A rebours* on precious stones by examining their Christian symbolism and providing thus finally "a jewelry of the beyond." In *La Cathédrale,* too, he carried his botanical study from *A rebours* into the realm of liturgical horticulture — and projected the earlier passages on profane perfumes into a study of the mystical emblems in the aromas of Church ritual.

Huysmans calls the passage on the mediaeval plain-chant in *A rebours* an important source of inspiration for his later books and especially for passages in *En route* and *L'Oblat.* In brief, he identifies *A rebours* as "an immediate preparation for my Catholic work which is found there in germ in its entirety." He adds that, in *A rebours,* he was trying "to open windows" to get some fresh air in his writing and to break through the limits of the novel form so as to make it a frame to hold more serious work. Finally, he was seeking to get rid of the usual plot (passion and woman), to concentrate on a single personage, and "at all cost to do something new."

The clear orientation of *A rebours* toward Catholicism remains still for Huysmans incomprehensible. He cannot explain the call for religion at the end of his novel. He understands up to a point what happened to him between 1891 and 1895 (that is, between *Là-bas* and *En route*), but nothing at all of what happened between 1884 and 1891 (between *A rebours* and *Là-bas*). *A rebours* appeared in 1884, and Huysmans set out for his conversion in a Trappist monastery in 1892. "Why," he writes, "how was I urged along on a way lost for me then in the night? I am absolutely unable to say. . . ."

A rebours aroused a great deal of violent criticism. The author was treated as an impressionistic misanthrope, and his hero as an imbecile and a maniac — even, as we have seen, as "a sort of human sacculus." Huysmans was attacked for not praising Vergil, he was advised to undertake hydrotherapy for the state of his health, and his book was called absolutely incomprehensible.

"In all this chaos," he writes in the concluding passage of his *Preface,* "a single writer saw clearly, Barbey d'Aurevilly, who moreover did not know me at all. In an article in the *Constitutionnel* dated July 28, 1884 and which has been reprinted in his volume *The Contemporary Novel* (1902) he wrote:

> 'After such a book, the author has only a choice between the mouth of a pistol or the foot of the Cross.'"

And Huysmans adds as his own last word: "I have made my choice." It would be hard to doubt his sincerity.

Huysmans had early been caught by opposites, drawn (as he once wrote to a friend) by the supernatural of evil into the supernatural of good: "The one derived from the other. With his hooked claw the devil drew me towards God." Thereafter, Huysmans learned much from his quiet hours with the Trappists; and, like Baudelaire, he came to realize the mysterious spiritual values in personal suffering.

Evelyn Underhill, whose finest book on mysticism we cited in an earlier lecture, has observed how hard it is for material philosophy to come very meaningfully to grips with the fact of pain, "which plunges like a sword through creation, leaving on one side cringing and degraded animals and on the other side heroes and saints." Huysmans accepted willingly at last the terrible pain of a cancer of the mouth from which he died; and his mind was filled finally with the idea of a mystical substitution in which his suffering perhaps served to expiate the sins of others, like the suffering born so bravely in the fifteenth century by the Blessed Lydwine of Schiedam of whose life he had written.

Chateaubriand, Huysmans' great predecessor in French decadence, had remarked at the end of his *Mémoires d'outre-tombe*:

> I have nothing now to do but sit down by the edge of my grave; thereafter I shall go down unafraid, my crucifix in my hand, into eternity.

Huysmans was not given to such personal lyricism; but his quiet statement is in its way almost as memorable when he writes to a friend in January of 1907:

> I have a vague intuition that I shall be led out of the paths of literature, and into the expiatory ways of suffering, until I come to die. The worst of it is that I haven't a very decided sense of vocation for that sort of life, but in the end I shall undoubtedly get into the way of it.

He died before the year was out.

And so the author of the book that "poisoned" Dorian Gray comes himself at last along dark paths, but by ways of the spirit, to "the consoling beacons of the ancient hope" that his decadent hero had despaired of finding. Huysmans, too, had gone along the decadent way; but he was never quite at home there. His true quest was on another path, which may explain the continuous sense of irony that one has in reading *A rebours* and which is surely the explanation of what is said in its hero's final despairing cry.

Huysmans is seen today as an important influence in the great Catholic literary revival in France. With him the decadent way had turned at last into the way of the Cross, as Barbey d'Aurevilly had anticipated that it might. Perhaps, then, Wilde was right to sense already in *A rebours* the ecstasies of the mediaeval saint along with the morbid confessions of a modern sinner. He may have been more perceptive in this than we have realized; for, as we now know, Wilde himself was to come at last through deep humiliation and suffering along a comparable route after his own earlier journey on the decadent way.

V

RACINE'S *PHÈDRE* AND THE TRIUMPH OF LIGHT

> "Tragique est la lumière."
> *Rouault*

Phèdre BY JEAN RACINE is for me the most exquisite of tragedies. There is greater scope in the best plays of Shakespeare and greater power in the masterpieces of Aeschylus and Sophocles; but for pure focus upon a tragic situation and sheer artistry in the catharsis at the last I know nothing comparable with this lovely play from the elegant age of Louis XIV.

Over the years, in reading *Phèdre* with students and in considering it from the varying perspectives afforded by their comments and papers and the observations of scholarly critics and my own growing sense of certain details and forces at work in the play, I have become more and more conscious of roots that reach deep below the scenes and of how remarkably the imaginative structural network of images and symbols and myths prepares one for the overwhelming impression at the last.

This afternoon I hope to show some of these elements at work and to suggest at least a few of the particular and sometimes shadowy forces that combine with neo-Classic principles to help make *Phèdre* a tragic drama of surviving power.

I

The tragedies of Racine are much more delicate mechanisms than the tragedies of Shakespeare and, in order to establish something of their nature, I propose first of all to examine the effects of a few important neo-Classic principles that highlight essential differences in the art of these two authors who are for me the greatest writers of tragedy since the Greeks.

The masterpieces of Racine differ so notably from those of Shakespeare that they seem essentially different in kind, and in many ways they are. It is not that we must choose one sort of tragedy over the other — it would be rather fatuous today to urge Racine and Shakespeare as rivals — but rather that each dramatist deserves admiration and understanding for his special qualities. There is, in fact, much more than academic interest involved in the differences between Racinian and Shakespearean tragedy, for they suggest quite different ways of seeing and of representing life itself.

Two basic concepts of French neo-Classic theory are insistence upon the so-called "three unities" of time, place and action and the separation of the dramatic genres. These concepts are in themselves responsible for much of the concentrated form and purity of French neo-Classic tragedy and are so crucial to an understanding of Racine's tragic art that I should like to consider their significance in some detail.

The concept of the three unities, which developed out of Italian commentaries on the *Poetics* of Aristotle during the Renaissance, exerted a powerful influence upon French neo-Classical dramaturgy. The ultimate statement about them in French theory is that of Boileau in his famous *Art poétique* that appeared in 1674, three years before the *Phèdre* of Racine; and Boileau's verses are known to every French schoolboy who has read French literature of the seventeenth century:

> Qu'en un lieu, qu'en un jour, un seul fait accompli
> Tienne jusqu'à la fin le théâtre rempli.

One almost smiles at hearing the familiar lines:

> Let a single act, in a single day, in one place
>   brought to completion
> Hold the stage filled until the end.

Yet this *cliché* sums up a key concept of the magnificent tragedy of seventeenth-century France.

The significance of the unities is evident when one considers in turn the plays of Shakespeare and of Racine. The Shakespearean hero has opportunities for character development through a series of varied experiences in time; and we can see the process at work as in, say, Macbeth or Lear. The Racinian hero or heroine, on the contrary, is seen over a period of only twenty-four hours or a little more, and character change must be shown, if at all, through flashbacks or other reference to the past. In Racinian drama, then, what we see is primarily character revelation rather than character development in the protagonist. Such limitation in time serves to concentrate French neo-Classic tragedy within a narrowed frame, where what is lost in breadth of action and character-play is in part compensated for by the very special kind of compression it allows.

The neo-Classic concept of separation of dramatic genres affords also in Racinian tragedy a fascinatingly different kind of drama from that of Shakespeare. According to this concept, tragedy should be purely tragic with no intrusion of comic or grotesque or humorous or vulgar elements. This allows a continuous purity of tone in the finest neo-Classic tragedies that is absent from the great tragedies of Shakespeare, some of whose most powerful effects depend, as in life itself, upon the mingling of these very elements.

Many of the most memorable scenes in Shakespeare's finest plays would have to be sacrificed if they were subjected to the neo-Classic rules of seventeenth-century France. *Macbeth* would lose, for example, its witches and its drunken porter and Birnam wood coming to Dunsinane; *Hamlet* would have to do without much of the memorable conversation with the ghost and the scene with the grave-diggers and the soliloquy over the skull of poor Yorick; in *Romeo and Juliet* the nurse would lose her racy and humorous character and there would be no Mercutio as we know him in the play; and in *King Lear* the great central figure would hardly be set to apostrophize as he does the storm-winds, thunder, rain and fire upon the heath and would surely not worry with a button at the last. Thus elements that make for much of the special power in Shakespeare's theatre would be almost wholly lost.

Then there is the matter of vocabulary. One of the most lively qualities in Shakespeare is his marvellously fresh language with its frequent puns, bawdy references and ambiguities, and general exuberance. Moreover, in Shakespeare's supreme command of native English speech, rhetoric and the most subtle empathic poetry interweave in dazzling word-play of a sort quite alien to the spirit and practice of French neo-Classicism. The tragic vocabulary of Shakespeare is remarkably free from restraint and embraces vividly the varied natural world outside of man. Racine's, on the contrary, is a subdued vocabulary of limited scope — the vocabulary of an aristocratic, urbane society whose concerns in literature were primarily with the moral, psychological, religious and established social aspects of man's nature and whose expression was controlled by the rules of a most elegant propriety or *bienséance*.

In brief, the art of Shakespeare and the art of Racine are all but mutually exclusive. It is our very great good fortune that the flourishing period of French neo-Classicism from about 1660 to 1685 came too late to influence Shakespeare. It seems to me equally fortunate for the literature of France that Shakespeare's genius did not affect the artistry of Racine.

II

There are of course many elements that combine in the creation of a great work of art. We noted in an earlier lecture of this series Baudelaire's idea that for a work to possess universality it must be animated by the accent of its time. We find this very clear in Racine's *Phèdre,* and it is as obviously the accent of the height of French Classicism as the accent in *Les Fleurs du Mal* is that of the post-Romantic nineteenth century in France. This contemporary and local quality is of great interest, and it tells us something of unusual value about human perspectives and ways of perception at a unique moment and place in human experience. But *Phèdre* transcends its age and the unique and elegant culture from which it came and, like all surviving great works of art, it speaks to us still as if somehow it enjoyed a miraculous life beyond the reach of time. Yet the beauty of *Phèdre* is all but inaccessible to those who cannot read its Alexandrine verses in Racine's original language. The play's essential artistry does not survive translation; and when in some far distant age the beautiful tongue in which it was written is no longer known, *Phèdre* will have perished with it.

Meanwhile, after nearly three centuries, fortunately and under-
standably, Racine's play is with us still.

*   *   *

The plot-line of *Phèdre* is very old, and Racine's main sources
for details and for much of the structure of his play are the
Hippolytus of Euripides and Seneca's *Phaedra*. Racine's adaptation
of his materials to French neo-Classical theory depends upon
numerous conventions of his day and upon his own exquisite genius.
But there are unexpected elements at work that may surprise a
reader with traditional conceptions of neo-Classic art. As background for our consideration of details in *Phèdre* I should like now
to examine briefly the matter of the tragic catharsis and then the
great archetypal symbols of the sea and light that we shall find so
intricately woven into the texture of Racine's masterpiece.

The idea of catharsis as a cleansing of the tragic emotions of
pity and fear is widely understood today to mean, not getting rid
of these emotions (for a human being without pity would be a
dangerous creature and one without fear might not long survive),
but of purging (i.e., purifying) the emotions themselves. (Racine
translates Aristotle's definition of tragedy as "une représentation,
qui excitant la pitié et la terreur, purge ces sortes de passions,"
which seems clearly to suggest purification of these emotions, rather
than getting rid of them completely.)

For my purpose I prefer to examine the catharsis in a somewhat
special way, stressing the importance of empathic experience, and
seeing the catharsis itself as resulting from a process analogous to
that at work in the play of successful metaphor. In such catharsis
the experience is immediately and primarily aesthetic, and the
didactic element survives as an aftermath of aesthetic perception.

There is an interesting discussion of ideas related to this matter
in James Joyce's *A Portrait of the Artist as a Young Man,* when
Stephen Dedalus in the presence of his companion Lynch is
examining the question of good and bad art. Stephen holds that
bad art is kinetic in its effects in that, for example, it sets
one rushing with lust toward something (as in pornographic art) or
rushing with loathing away from something (as in immediately
didactic art). The effect of good art, on the contrary, is static, in

the sense that it puts the soul in a state of *stasis,* in which, having risen above immediate ordinary contingencies, it experiences a moment of illumination "above desire and loathing."

This seems to me a very useful analysis of the function of great metaphor as well as of successful catharsis in great narrative or drama. For a privileged moment, thanks to the overwhelming aesthetic power of the poetry or of the narrative or dramatic art, we rise free, as it were, from the particular contingencies of ordinary life (even as they exist in the work whose power we feel) and, in a kind of aesthetic *stasis,* stand above the viewpoints of usual perspective and are enabled to see, for a moment, clear and far. This is the kind of artistic triumph that I hope to show at the last in *Phèdre.*

Ideally, the tragic protagonist should experience the catharsis along with the resultant privileged vision; and the audience or reader should share empathically in both the experience and the vision at the last through the aesthetic power of the tragic art. I see Racine as having accomplished this in *Phèdre* in a way unique in tragic literature; and the process involves all the elements with which we have thus far been concerned and something else besides.

An unusually important aspect of Racine's art in *Phèdre* is his employment of the great archetypal symbols of the sea and light. The sea is a recurrent image in literature for the infinite and for eternity. It is also a great female image. Consciousness of the sea's proximity seems to exert very generally a remarkable influence upon the human imagination; and its mystery and vastness and ageless variety make it one of the most powerful and emotionally evocative of all the great primordial natural forces.

The ancient Greeks knew the strangeness and beauty and mystery of the sea. It lay around them, and they had the feel of its waters. For Homer it was "wine-dark" and "many-roaring," and Aeschylus describes the "boundless (*or* innumerable) laughter" of its waves. In the *Odyssey* the Greeks have given us the greatest of all sea adventures; and Odysseus himself, the greatest of sea-farers, is destined according to a late interpretation of Tiresias' prophecy, to have death come to him finally from the sea when Telegonus, his son by Circe, will kill him with a spear whose tip is the bone of a sea-fish.

The sea seems to be forever present in *Phèdre*; and the dark forces from ancient mythology are seen over and over coming from its waters until it appears that much of the tragedy in the play is native to this ancient element.

Venus, the Goddess of Love, was born of the sea foam *(aphros),* as is evident in her Greek name Aphrodite, and according to Lemprière she has numerous other names that proclaim her goddess of the sea: Pontia, Marina, Limnesia, Epipontia, Pelagia, Saligenia, Pontogenia, Aligena, Thalassia, and Anadyomene (literally, "rising [from the sea]").

Neptune (the Greek Poseidon) is of crucial pertinence here as the God of the Sea. He is credited with creating the horse, and a horse and a bull were generally sacrificed upon his altars by the ancients. The background relation with the tragedy of Phaedra is here especially significant for, according to a widely accepted tradition, the bull with which Phaedra's mother, Pasiphaë, fell in love and through which she gave birth to the Minotaur, had been given to King Minos by Neptune for sacrifice on the altar of the god. Minos, because of the animal's beauty, refused to carry out the sacrifice, and Neptune avenged himself by arousing the bestial lust in Pasiphaë that was to lead to so much woe and misery in so many lives.

The great archetypal symbols of light and darkness also play their antiphonal roles in *Phèdre*. The heroine herself is a daughter of Minos, one of the judges in the dark Underworld; but on her mother's side she is the granddaughter of the Sun (Helios), and there is a subtle playing off of darkness against light in Racine's dramatic imagery.

Recognition of a symbolic relationship between purity and light is recurrent in tradition and in literature. One can perhaps see an aspect of this in Shelley's famous image from his "Adonais" on the death of Keats:

> Life, like a dome of many-coloured glass,
> Stains the white radiance of Eternity,
> Until Death tramples it to fragments.

And this sense of the image is clearly evident in the statement from Jewish legend that if one had been present at the creation before the clouding influence of sin he would have found the celestial light so clear that he could have seen at a single glance all the way across the world. This celestial light was one of seven precious gifts enjoyed by Adam before the fall, in which it was lost to man, to whom it will not be granted again until the Messianic time. We shall see how an aspect of this ancient light symbolism has been woven with exquisite art into the essential structure of Racine's greatest tragedy.

III

We have noted briefly something of the concentrated framework within which the tragic action in Racine's plays must evolve and the narrow radius of his tragic vocabulary; and we have seen the importance of certain elements in ancient myth with which Racine was concerned and the archetypal significance of two of his major images. It should be useful now to examine in some detail the marvellous way in which these elements are controlled and ordered and brought together in the development of the play itself; and it is to this that we shall turn now at the last.

*   *   *

There are only 1654 lines in the five acts of Racine's *Phèdre,* and Quemada's recent concordance gives a total vocabulary of a mere 1653 different words in the whole play — one less than the number of lines! Key words include such inwardly-directed terms as *innocence . . . duty . . . suffering . . . despair . . . remorse . . . love . . . shame . . . fear . . . flight . . . reason . . .* and *fury.* In Racine's text the French words *silence* and *cacher* (to hide or keep secret) recur with implication of hidden things that the characters would keep concealed — things that should not be heard or seen. A careful study of such words would underline the intense psychological and moral stresses and strains within the characters and between and among them as the play unfolds. But this afternoon I wish to take a different direction and show, as suggested earlier, some of the larger patterns of force in the structure of the play by stressing a few recurrent words, deities and symbols that play a somewhat different role. I have chosen for this the words *monster* and *poison,* * the divinities Venus and Neptune, sunlight and darkness, and the image of the great sea.

As the play begins, Hippolytus and his tutor Theramenes are discussing Hippolytus' plans for leaving Troezene to seek his father Theseus who has been gone for over six months. They fear that he may be dead; but Theramenes says that he himself has already crossed several seas in a vain search for Theseus. Reference to "the sea that saw Icarus fall" introduces early the ominous symbol of the Labyrinth, which stands horribly in the background suggesting the maze in which all the characters of the play will seem, in a sense, to be wandering before the end. Theramenes observes that Theseus, so long fickle in love, may be enjoying a new love-affair; but Hippolytus protests. He says he will merely follow his duty in seeking his father, and he will be fleeing from a region where he fears to dwell. When Theramenes asks what is driving him from a place he has loved since childhood, Hippolytus replies with words that introduce at once a tone of deep sadness into the play and that recall Phèdre's fearful heritage:

> Cet heureux temps n'est plus. Tout a changé de face
> Depuis que sur ces bords les Dieux ont envoyé
> La fille de Minos et de Pasiphaé.

> [That happy time is no more. Everything has changed
> Since the Gods sent to these shores
> The daughter of Minos and Pasiphaë.]

But when Theramenes pursues the matter further, we learn that Hippolytus is really fleeing from his love for Aricia, the last of a rival family with a claim to the throne of Athens. Theseus had killed all her brothers and spared her with the injunction that she was never to marry. Hippolytus rightly feels guilt at his love for Aricia, for it could endanger the stability of the Athenian state.

Aricia is a new character, introduced by Racine. She has no role in the plays of Euripides and Seneca. Racine says that he took her from Vergil; but a subtle touch is evident (whether Racine was

---

* For ideas on the structural and metaphorical use of these two words in *Phèdre* I am indebted to the fine article by Robert W. Hartle, "Racine's Hidden Metaphors," *Modern Language Notes,* LXXVI (February 1961), 132-139.

conscious of it or not) in the fact that Aricia is one of the names of Diana (the Greek Artemis of Euripides' tragedy), who is mentioned only once in Racine's play and then only in an insignificant reference.

In his discussion with Theramenes Hippolytus introduces the motif of monsters, which will be so important as the play develops. He refers to the monsters slain by Theseus and mentions among them "Crete reeking with the blood of the Minotaur." The image of this monstrous creature that was Phèdre's half-brother thus serves already to set in shadowy outline the framework of monstrous heredity of which Phèdre feels herself a victim.

Hippolytus tells us of his unhappiness at his father's numerous love-affairs, but declares that in loving he would be less excusable than Theseus since no monsters have yet been destroyed by his action. Moreover, can he be so rash as to love someone whose marriage his father has forbidden?

Theramenes urges Hippolytus not to be afraid of a chaste love and points out that Venus has overcome many noble hearts — Hercules and even Hippolytus' mother, the Amazon queen Antiope. Theramenes has noticed that for some time now Hippolytus has not been hunting or taming horses, an art he identifies as having been invented by the sea-god, Neptune. Can it be that Hippolytus is in love with Aricia?

Hippolytus avoids answering, saying that he is leaving to look for Theseus and that he will see Phèdre before he goes. As he speaks, Oenone (Phèdre's nurse) is seen approaching in great distress, and the first scene of the tragedy ends on this note.

In less than 150 lines we have already clear suggestion of major forces at work in the play — the sea itself and its deity Neptune, who is the creator of the horse and the god of taming horses — Venus, the goddess of love, born from the foam of the sea — the theme of monsters and the monstrous Minotaur, half-brother of Phèdre, born to Pasiphaë in punishment for her husband's affront to the sea-god — and the ominous Labyrinth, most intricate and famous of mazes, in which the Minotaur was housed until it was killed by Theseus. It is notable, too, that Hippolytus' name means "looser of horses" and that Hippolytus is skilled in the horse-taming art invented by the god of the sea.

Oenone tells Hippolytus that Phèdre is dying of some hidden illness. She is coming out now to see the daylight once more after sending her other attendants away. Phèdre appears on stage in the third scene, and her first speech, full of profound sadness, concerns the light of the sun. She is so weak that she can hardly walk and in distracted words complains of her weakness and the hostile world around her. Then, in a despairing apostrophe, she addresses her ancestor, the sun:

> Noble and brillant auteur d'une triste famille,
> Toi, dont ma mère osait se vanter d'être fille,
> Qui peut-être rougis du trouble où tu me vois,
> Soleil, je te viens voir pour la dernière fois.

> [Noble and brilliant author of an unhappy family,
> You, of whom my mother dared boast of being the daughter,
> Who perhaps blush at the confusion in which you see me,
> O Sun, I come to look upon you for the last time.]

Here the close relationship is established between Phèdre and the sun-god and, in more human terms, the symbolic relationship between Phèdre and *le jour* (the light of day).

When Oenone questions her, Phèdre replies incoherently and longs to see again a chariot fleeing through a cloud of dust. Oenone seeks an explanation of this strange reference, and Phèdre says the gods have made her lose control of her mind and her desires so that, in spite of herself, she has revealed her shameful suffering.

Oenone asks what charm or what poison has done this to Phèdre. She pleads the cause of Phèdre's children who, if their mother dies, will lose their rights to that proud enemy of Phèdre's race, the son of the Amazon woman — Hippolytus.

Phèdre cries out in anguish at hearing the name and, when Oenone keeps questioning her, says she has lived too long already in her guilt. Oenone begs Phèdre to tell her secret and kneels, in the pleading posture of the suppliant that had such power over the Greek imagination. Phèdre tells her nurse at last that she will be horrified if Phèdre's silence is broken. She recalls the hatred of Venus that had destroyed her mother and her sister, and says that, because of Venus, she herself is dying the last and most wretched of her unhappy line.

When Oenone asks quite simply, "Are you in love?" Phèdre replies, "I have all the mad longings of love." And she tries to avoid saying Hippolytus' name. "I love . . ." —"Whom?" —"You know that son of the Amazon Woman, that Prince so long oppressed by me?" —"Hippolytus? Great Gods!" —And Phèdre, seeking to keep a little silence still, replies: "C'est toi qui l'a nommé." ("It is you who pronounced his name.")

Phèdre recalls then how she first saw Hippolytus not long after her marriage to Theseus. The symptoms of her love (alternate blush and pallor, confusion, indistinct vision and loss of speech, by turns a chill and a fever) told her at once that Venus was at work with her terrible passions. She burned offerings on Venus's altars to appease the goddess, but found herself calling instead upon the name of Hippolytus. She avoided him, only to find his features in those of his father. Finally, pretending to be a jealous step-mother, she had Hippolytus sent into exile. This afforded temporary relief until Theseus himself brought her back to Troezene, where she saw Hippolytus once more. The wound of love again broke open, and Phèdre characterizes its effect in words that are often seen to sum up the play:

> Ce n'est plus une ardeur dans mes veines cachée:
> C'est Vénus toute entière à sa proie attachée.
>
> [It is no more a burning hidden in my veins:
> It is Venus in all her power attached to her prey.]

And the phrase "Vénus toute entière" seems here to have the terrible meaning of "stark lust."

Phèdre tells of the just terror she conceived for her crime and of how she came to hate life and to hold her passion in horror. We can see in her words her admiration for the pure light of the sun, her ancestor.

> Je voulais en mourant prendre soin de ma gloire,
> Et dérober au jour une flamme si noire ...
>
> [I wanted to preserve my honor by dying,
> And to steal from the light of day so dark a passion ...]

She asks now only that Oenone leave her alone in her resolve for death.

Then unexpectedly comes the report that Theseus is dead. Oenone insists that Phèdre can now see her step-son without any guilt and urges that she join with Hippolytus to oppose the claims of Aricia to the throne of Athens.

In a moment of terrible weakness at the end of the first act Phèdre allows her servant to make her decisions for her.

* * *

In Act Two we hear various accounts of how Theseus probably met his death. One is that he drowned at sea — another that he had descended to the underworld with his friend Pirithous and could not again cross over "the shores that one crosses without return."

Hippolytus comes to free Aricia from her long bondage and to restore to her the rule of Athens. Then, without quite intending to do so, he reveals his love; and he does this in figurative language referring to the sea. He has lost all pleasure in hunting and in his chariot — he has forgotten Neptune's lessons and (a point crucial in the fate of Hippolytus) his idle steeds have forgotten the sound of his voice.

Hippolytus takes leave of Aricia as Phèdre is seen approaching. She has come to ask Hippolytus' help for her children; but at sight of him she forgets what she came to say. She tries to explain that her apparent unfriendliness was not at all what it seemed — that she was not a jealous step-mother, as he must have thought. A very different concern is responsible for her confusion.

Hippolytus attempts to reassure her. It is not yet time to be so troubled. Theseus may still see the light of day. And Hippolytus adds, in a passage whose terrible irony is not yet apparent, that Theseus is protected by Neptune, who will surely answer his prayers.

Then comes the magnificent psychological stroke in which Racine shows us Phèdre's mind shifting without ever quite meaning to do so to the revelation of her love. We should recall here Phèdre's earlier confession to her nurse that when she tried to forget Hippolytus she found his features again in the face of Theseus. Now the fatal process is reversed.

Phèdre replies to Hippolytus that there can be no further doubt about Theseus' death:

One does not see the shore of the dead twice,
My lord. Since Theseus has seen those dark shores,
You will hope in vain for a god to send him back to you;
Greedy Acheron does not give up its prey.
What am I saying? He is not dead, since he still breathes in you.
Still before my eyes I seem to see my husband.
I see him, I speak to him; and my heart. . . . My mind is wandering,
My lord, my mad passion in spite of me speaks out.

Hippolytus seeks to interpret this as referring to Phèdre's love for
Theseus, even though he is dead; and Phèdre, gradually losing all
control of her emotions, develops his suggestion in one of the most
powerful passages in French drama:

> Oui, Prince, je languis, je brûle pour Thésée.
> Je l'aime. . . .

> [Yes, Prince, I languish, I burn with longing for Theseus.
> I love him. . . .]

Phèdre describes the Theseus that she loves — a Theseus faithful
and proud, a little fierce, godlike in appearance, like Hippolytus
himself. She recalls that when Theseus came across the waves to
Crete he resembled Hippolytus in bearing, eyes, speech, and mod-
esty of expression — a worthy object for the desires of Minos's
daughters.

   Then, as her mind shifts completely to Hippolytus, Phèdre continues with words of overwhelming passion that move from image
to image in her terrible past and show us, indeed, "Venus in all
her power attached to her prey."

> What were you doing then? Why, without Hippolytus,
> Did [Theseus] assemble the finest heroes of Greece?
> Why, too young still, could you not then
> Have entered the ship that put him on our shores?
> Through you the monster of Crete would have perished,
> In spite of the turns of his vast retreat.
> To lead you through its confused passageways
> My sister with the fatal thread would have armed your hand.
> But no, I would have preceded her there:
> Love would have made me think of it first.
> It is I, Prince, it is I whose useful aid
> Would have taught you the turns of the Labyrinth.
> What cares that charming head would have cost me!

A thread would not have been enough for your lover.
Companion in the peril that you had to seek,
I myself would have wished to go before you;
And Phèdre, descended with you into the Labyrinth,
Would have been with you saved or lost.

Hippolytus, horrified, pretends not to understand; but Phèdre says he has understood only too well. And she admits all the frenzy of her love, telling how she has fought against its poison — how she loathes herself even more than Hippolytus detests her. It is the gods who have kindled in her the passion that is fatal to all her line. As for the shameful admission of her love, does he think it was voluntary? She had meant to speak to him in behalf of her son but could speak at last only of the one she loved. And she calls upon Hippolytus to destroy her:

Worthy son of the hero who gave you the light of day,
Free the universe from a troubling monster.
The widow of Theseus dares love Hippolytus!
Believe me, this frightful monster must not escape you.
There is my heart. It is there that your hand must strike.
… … … … …
Strike. Or if you think it unworthy of your blows,
If you hate me so much that such punishment is too slight,
Or if your hand would be stained in too vile a blood,
For lack of your hand, lend me your sword.
Give it to me.

As Theramenes approaches, Oenone leads Phèdre away. Hippolytus flees with his tutor, leaving his fallen sword behind. He prays that the horrible secret he has discovered will remain forever buried in deep oblivion.

Theramenes says that Athens has declared itself for Phèdre, but that there is a vague report that Theseus has been seen alive.

* * *

In the third act Phèdre sends Oenone to tempt Hippolytus with the crown of Athens. She is to assume a suppliant tone if she must. Phèdre will put both herself and her son in Hippolytus' power. She confides all her hopes to Oenone's mission. Then, in a scene alone, Phèdre calls in her anguish upon the goddess of Love, who is responsible for her misery:

> O you, who see the shame to which I have descended,
> Implacable Venus, am I sufficiently humbled?
> You could not drive your cruelty farther.
> Your triumph is perfect; all your arrows have gone home.

She calls upon Venus to attack Hippolytus, who has never knelt at her altars. But Oenone's return puts an end to the prayer.

Oenone reports that Theseus is alive and has arrived in Troezene, and Phèdre is in despair at what she has revealed of her passion. Even if Hippolytus keeps silence, Phèdre knows her guilt. In dying she will be free — but she trembles at thought of her children's suffering from her lost honor.

Oenone imagines Hippolytus telling Phèdre's shame and asks how Phèdre sees him now. Phèdre's reply keeps alive a pattern of significant imagery: "I see him as a monster frightful in my eyes." Then why not accuse him first? says Oenone. Seeing Phèdre's horror at the idea, Oenone says that all she asks is silence from her mistress. Theseus will not punish his son severely — and besides to save Phèdre's honor "one must sacrifice everything, even virtue." But someone is coming. Oenone says that she sees Theseus. And Phèdre replies:

> Ah! I see Hippolytus:
> In his insolent eyes I see my fate written.
> Do what you wish, I give in to you.
> In my confused state, I can do nothing for myself.

When Theseus arrives, he finds Phèdre aloof and embarrassed, claiming that he has been wronged and that she is unworthy to approach him. Theseus wonders why under such circumstances heaven freed him from his prison. He tells how he had unwillingly tried to help his friend Pirithous in a love affair, and how the two had been captured by the woman's husband. Pirithous had been fed by the tyrant to cruel monsters, and the tyrant himself had suffered the same fate when Theseus finally escaped and avenged his friend's death. Theseus cannot understand what has happened. And Hippolytus at the end of the third act wonders what his father will say when he finds the truth. Even Theseus cannot shake his love for Aricia; but Hippolytus thinks: "What a terrible poison Love has spread over all his house!"

*   *   *

In Act Four Oenone accuses Hippolytus of violence against Phèdre and of preparing to kill her with his sword. Oenone tells Theseus that Hippolytus' criminal love was the cause of Phèdre's hatred. When Hippolytus asks Theseus what is wrong, his father calls him a monster and links him with the brigands Theseus had destroyed long before. In growing anger, he speaks brutally to his son, tells him to flee from the land into exile, and finally calls down upon him the wrath of Neptune, the sea-god. Hippolytus, in horror, tries to defend himself. He pleads finally that "the light of day is not more pure than the depths of my heart" — and we see one of Racine's beautiful structural images reappearing in the phrase. But Theseus is deaf to his son's defense; and, when Hippolytus confesses his love for Aricia, Theseus acuses him of pretending another treachery in self-justification. He banishes his son with bitter words and, as he sees him leave, speaks an ominous soliloquy:

> Wretched creature, you run to your inevitable doom.
> Neptune, by the river terrible even to the Gods,
> Has given me his word and will carry it out.
> An avenging God follows you . . .

Hearing the angry voice of Theseus, Phèdre comes, apparently intending to confess her guilt; but when she learns from Theseus that Hippolytus has said he loves Aricia, she is struck speechless. Later, in a scene with Oenone, she laments her new jealous agony as she thinks of the young lovers:

> Heaven approved the innocence of their sighs;
> They followed their love without remorse;
> Every day rose clear and serene for them.
> And I, wretched outcast of all nature,
> I hid myself from the light of day, I fled from the light . . .

Then, after crying aloud for Aricia's destruction, Phèdre checks herself in horror:

> My crimes now have gone beyond all measure.
> I breathe out at once incest and imposture.
> My murderous hands, prompt to avenge me,
> Burn with desire to be plunged in innocent blood.
> O wretched! and I live? and I endure the sight
> Of that sacred sun from which I am descended?
> I have for grandfather the father and master of the Gods:
> The heavens, the whole universe is full of my ancestors.
> Where can I hide? Let me flee into infernal night.
> But what am I saying? my father holds there the fatal urn . . .

And she imagines Minos trembling when he hears his daughter forced to admit crimes that are perhaps unknown in hell.

When Oenone tries, as she has tried before, to excuse Phèdre's human weakness, her mistress turns upon her at last in fury, accuses her of what she has done to Hippolytus, and says she will listen no more. Calling Oenone a "hateful monster" [*monstre exécrable*], Phèdre banishes her with a curse:

> Go, leave to me the care of my deplorable fate.
> May just heaven repay you as you deserve!
> And may your punishment for ever terrify
> All those who, like you, by base craft,
> Nourish the weakness of unhappy Princes,
> Urge them along the descent where their heart is inclined,
> And dare smooth for them the path of crime,
> Detestable deceivers, the most baneful present
> That celestial wrath can give to kings!

And Oenone by herself at the last says only:

> Oh, Gods! I have done everything, left everything behind
> [to serve her;
> And this is my reward? I have really deserved it.

* * *

The last act of *Phèdre* moves rapidly to its tragic end. Hippolytus urges Aricia to leave Troezene, "where virtue breathes a poisoned air." The lovers agree to meet at the city gates, amidst the ancient tombs of Hippolytus' ancestors. There in a holy temple they will confirm the vow of their love. Hippolytus will call upon the name of chaste Diana and august Juno, and all the gods will be witness to his faith.

Hippolytus leaves as Theseus approaches; and Aricia tells the king that he has destroyed innumerable monsters but that he is leaving one still alive. . . . She goes no further because of her promise to Hippolytus that she would keep silence about Phèdre's shame. When Aricia leaves, Theseus begins at last to wonder and asks that Oenone be brought to him for further questioning.

But it is too late. Theseus learns that Phèdre is beside herself and near death and that Oenone, driven from the Queen's presence, has drowned herself in the sea. Theseus calls then for Hippolytus to come and defend himself; and he entreats Neptune not to hasten the granting of his prayer to destroy his son.

Once again it is too late. Theramenes has already arrived with the report of Hippolytus' death, which is recounted in the famous *récit de Théramène,* one of the most famous passages in French literature.

Theramenes tells how Hippolytus set out in his chariot on the road to Mycenae and exile. His horses seemed to share his sorrow and went sadly along the way. Then suddenly a terrible cry arose from the depths of the sea. A mountainous wave approached, broke, and hurled forth a furious monster amidst the sea-foam. Its body was covered with yellowish scales, but there were horns on its wide forehead and it is called both dragon and bull.

The monster shakes the earth and infects the air, and the wave that had brought it recedes in terror. Everyone flees but Hippolytus, who hurls a javelin and makes a great wound in the monster's side. The creature leaps up and falls roaring before the horses, rolls over and covers them with fire, blood and smoke. In terror the horses run away, deaf now to Hippolytus' voice. It is said even that a god was seen urging the fleeing horses on with goads. The axle of the chariot breaks and Hippolytus falls tangled in the reins and is dragged horribly to his death.

Finally the horses stop near the ancient tombs of Hippolytus' ancestors, where he and Aricia were to have met. The dying hero proclaims his innocence and asks that Aricia be cared for after his death and that, if Theseus ever learns the truth, to appease his dead son's ghost he treat his captive gently. Death cuts short Hippolytus' final words. He is so disfigured that when Aricia arrives she can hardly recognize him and falls fainting before his torn body. Theramenes says that he has come, detesting the light of day, to bring Hippolytus' dying request to Theseus. As he speaks, Phèdre is seen approaching.

Theseus tells Phèdre that she has triumphed. Hippolytus is dead. He will consider his son a criminal, since Phèdre accuses him; but she must let Theseus go now far from her and far from Troezene to seek oblivion in an alien land.

But Phèdre has come to proclaim Hippolytus' innocence. She has only a few moments left and calls upon Theseus to listen to her words. She confesses her lust, which she sees as incestuous, blames heaven for stirring desire within her, and tells of Oenone's lying accusation. Oenone has sought in the waves a punishment that Phèdre considers too mild for her betrayal. Phèdre would already have killed herself with a sword; but she wished before her death to reveal her remorse to Theseus and to restore honor to his dead son.

Phèdre has taken poison and she dies as she speaks her last lines. It is Theseus' words that end the play, when he would have the memory of Phèdre's action perish with her, tells of his intention of honoring Hippolytus, and promises to accept Aricia as his daughter. But the tragedy's aesthetic dénouement is really in the last words of Phèdre:

> I have taken, I have caused to flow in my burning veins
> A poison that Medea brought into Athens.
> Already the venom reaching my heart
> In this dying heart hurls an unknown cold;
> Already I see no more except through a cloud
> The sky and the husband whom my presence shames;
> And death, stealing the light from my eyes,
> Gives back to the light of day, that they sullied,
>   all its purity.

*   *   *

The monsters that recur so often in abstract or somewhat oblique reference through the play prefigure the material monster that rises at last from the sea — the bull-like creature sent by the sea-god to destroy Hippolytus. And the monster recalls and is clearly related to the bull in the monstrous legend of Minos and Pasiphaë that is so terrible a part of Phèdre's and Theseus' destinies.

The poisons that recur in so many abstract references appear at last concretely in the poison brought over the sea by the great sorceress Medea — the poison that Phèdre takes for her suicide. Thus, in the tragedy, the emerging monster is responsible for the death of Hippolytus and the emerging poison for the death of Phèdre, and both come through a kind of remorseless aesthetic logic by way of the sea to fulfill their tragic roles.

In like manner Phèdre's final words bring the play to its tragic focus at the last. Of all the characters I know in literature Racine's Phèdre has the greatest longing for purity, and her dying word is *pureté*. Moreover, in Phèdre's last two lines all the light symbolism of the play is brought to its exquisite fulfilment in her words on purified light that furnish so perfectly the magnificent catharsis of this greatest of French tragedies:

> Et la mort, à mes yeux dérobant la clarté,
> Rend au jour qu'ils souillaient toute sa pureté.

There is another image, too, unspecified, but it seems to me essential at the last — an image that concerns the sea. We have seen how much of the tragedy comes from the sea: the influence of Neptune and of sea-born Venus — the bull of Crete that was to have been sacrificed to the sea-god — the many journeys over waters — the poison brought across the sea by Medea — the death sought by Oenone in the waves — the monstrous sea-bull (rising like Venus herself amidst the sea-foam) that was responsible for the death of Hippolytus, who was himself skilled in the sea-god's art and destroyed by it and by his horses, the creatures of Neptune. The presence of the curse seems to me as evident in the sea as in the clouded light of the sun; and it is notable that Racine alone of the three dramatists we have cited as writing on this theme has Hippolytus wound the monster that comes against his horses from the sea. The creature falls, as we have seen, roaring and bleeding before his javelin; and it seems clear that Racine must have associated this sea-creature (which shook the earth and infected the air and caused the wave to recede in terror before it) with the curse upon Phèdre that sullied the light of day, and thus seen it as fouling all the elements.

I would see here one further detail — not specified by Racine, but implied in his exquisite imagery. I would see the death of the monster in the sea at the very moment of Phèdre's death. And the catharsis — the tragic cleansing — would thus be in terms of all four of the elements, but most dramatically in terms of the sea and the light of day. And so, at the last, after the longing and tragic purification and death of Phèdre, the granddaughter of the Sun, we see, through the purified air and over the purified earth and waters, the white sunlight shining on once more in "all its purity."

VI

"THYME, THAT CHEF OF SEASONERS":
ON TIME AND ITS IMAGES IN LITERATURE

TIME IS THE SILENT, intangible, unseen medium in which we live and die. Plato in the *Timaeus* calls it "a moving image of eternity," and this, too, is part of its mystery. We conceive of many kinds of time — and before all others, since it is most habitual to the majority of us, the time of our everyday chronometers and calendars, where we gauge time's passing in the familiar terms of seconds, minutes, hours, days, weeks, months, years, decades, centuries, and millennia. In such reckoning, as Professor Harlow Shapley once wrote, "our time thoughts are conditioned by the rotation of Planet Number 3 in the solar system" and are thus peculiarly parochial; but this really makes no difference to mankind, for however we reckon time its passing leaves us finally exposed in the same essentially lonely and human situation.

In the austere mathematics of science we think of the time of dinosaurs, mighty rivers, canyons, glaciers, mountains, seas, and stars — and we hear our astronomers speak of penetrating two billion light years into space with their great cameras and telescopes. Nor is this concept of vast time anything new to the imaginative minds of men. Long before human eyes had seen through telescopes and cameras, Lucretius had written of these matters in the first book of his *De Rerum Natura* [I. 999-1007]:

> Always the business of the universe is going on with incessant motion in every part, and the elements of matter are being supplied from beneath rushing from infinite space. Therefore the nature of space and the extent of the

deep is so great, that neither bright lightnings can traverse it in their course, though they glide onwards through endless tracts of time; nor can they by all their travelling make their journey any the less to go: so widely spreads the great store of space in the universe all around without limit in every direction. *

Thus, even in the world of materialist thought, the idea of "endless tracts of time" had not waited for modern science.

For religious mystics there has been also from ancient times the apprehension of eternity itself — the timelessness including and beyond all time, the dwelling-place of God and of the immortal soul of man.

All this makes the seventy years or so traditionally allotted to mankind in this world seem a very small spot of time indeed. Yet in this so-restricted period of earthly human time occur the subtle variations of the mind's chronology — in dreams and sleep and waking; in illusions and hallucinations; in pain and joy and fear and hope and sorrow; in waiting; and in the marvellous fields of memory.

These varying aspects of human perception and conception of time suffuse man's consciousness and relate to many other elements of his experience. In a sense, as Joyce has phrased it, man spends his life "seeking spoor through the deep timefield."

It is a notable evidence of the singular power in literature that moments or imaginings it captures for a while from time can so vividly survive in later years. Who can read in the *Iliad* [XXII. 387-390], for example, the grief-stricken cry of Achilles over his dead friend Patroclus and not sense its immediacy and its pertinence still to the human situation:

"I shall not forget him so long as I abide among the living and my knees are quick. If even in the house of Hades men forget their dead, yet even there shall I remember my dear comrade."

---

* The translations from Homer, Pindar, Lucretius, Horace, Tibullus, and Augustine are mostly from the Loeb Classical Library editions with minor changes; those from Aeschylus' *Agamemnon* are from the version of Richmond Lattimore; the Sappho is from Henry T. Wharton, and the Proust from the Random House translation by C. K. Scott Moncrieff and Frederick A. Blossom.

In like manner, as one reads Sappho's verses in her moon poem on the passing of time, it is hard to believe that they tell of the loneliness in the night of a beautiful spirit now dead for twenty-five centuries:

> The moon has set, and the Pleiades;
> it is midnight, the time is going by,
> and I sleep alone.

These are words we seem to overhear from the very moment we read them. Yet the thought of all those centuries and of Sappho so long dead enhances immeasurably the verses' power and their solemn, human pertinence in time.

The shock of immediacy is similar in the passage near the end of François Villon's *Lesser Testament* when suddenly, from the year 1456, we hear the bell called Marie ringing at the Sorbonne in the bitterly cold Parisian night. In Villon's words:

> Finablement, en escripvant,
> Ce soir. . . .
> ... ...
> J'oïs la cloche de Serbonne,
> Qui toujours à neuf heures sonne
> Le Salut que l'Ange predit. . . .
>
> [Finally, while writing
> This evening. . . .
> ... ...
> I hear the Sorbonne bell
> That always at the ninth hour rings
> The Salvation the Angel foretold. . . .]

The bell called Marie has long been silent; but, almost as the poet himself heard it near his room in the cold winter season, one can still hear this mediaeval bell as he reads the passage in which Villon wrote of it over half a thousand years ago.

And so it is that poets have claimed or been seen in a sense to conquer time. Thus Horace writes in the famous last poem of the third book of his *Odes* that he will not wholly die — that a great part of him will escape Libitina, the death-goddess, because, in his verse, he has completed a monument more lasting than bronze. And thus Samuel Johnson writes many centuries later that "the

stream of time ... passes without injury by the adamant of Shakespeare." But, in fact, it is relatively only a handful of years that
any poet can survive, for even the tongues in which men sing their
finest songs are lost in passing time.

Time has been considered from many points of view and in
relation to many disciplines. But tonight I propose to consider time,
not primarily from the viewpoint of philosophical ideas, but from
that of the variety of man's attitudes, moods, and images as they
are seen in the literature with which I am most familiar that is
concerned with this peculiarly mysterious element in our universe.

*   *   *

"*Quid est enim tempus?* For what is time?" writes Augustine
in his *Confessions.* "Who is able easily and briefly to explain that?
Who is able so much as in thought to comprehend it, so as to
express himself concerning it? And yet what in our usual discourse
do we more familiarly and knowingly make mention of than time?
And surely, we understand it well enough, when we speak of it:
we understand it also, when in speaking with another we hear
it named. What is time then? If nobody asks me, I know: but if I
were desirous to explain it to one that should ask me, plainly I know
not." [Book XI, xiv]

In mystical language, the tenses of man's mortal speech are
used to express the timeless element of his God: "Before Abraham
was I am" [John 8.58] — while at the beginning of Genesis is the
passage, called "sublime" by an ancient critic, which describes
God's creation of the basic time-scheme that we know:

> 1 In the beginning God created the heaven and the earth.
> 2 And the earth was without form, and void; and darkness
> was upon the face of the deep. And the Spirit of God
> moved upon the face of the waters. 3 And God said,
> Let there be light: and there was light. 4 And God
> saw the light, that it was good: and God divided the light
> from the darkness. 5 And God called the light Day, and
> the darkness he called Night. And the evening and the
> morning were the first day.

In the Biblical account this was five days before the creation of
man by the timeless Creator, whom Isaiah describes [57.15] as

"the high and lofty one that inhabiteth eternity, whose name is Holy. ...." From such concepts of time and timelessness and their developing relations with mankind come the laments of Job and the rapt expressions of Augustine — the Christian duality of mortal and immortal man.

In Job we find several of man's great, sad statements on the human condition in time: "Are not my days few? cease then, and let me alone, that I may take comfort a little. Before I go whence I shall not return, even to the land of darkness and the shadow of death; A land of darkness, as darkness itself; and of the shadow of death, without any order, and where the light is as darkness." [X. 20-22] And again: "[My days] are passed away as the swift ships; as the eagle that hasteth to the prey." [IX. 26] "For I know that thou wilt bring me to death, and to the house appointed for all living." [XXX. 23] "Man that is born of a woman, is of few days, and full of trouble. He cometh forth like a flower, and is cut down: he fleeth also as a shadow, and continueth not." [XIV. 1-2] With Augustine, it was different, as we shall see hereafter.

Flaubert remarks in a strange passage of his correspondence from which we quoted in an earlier lecture that . . .

> The melancholy of antiquity seems . . . more profound than that of the moderns, all of whom more or less conceive of immortality beyond the *black void* [le *trou noir*]. But, for the ancients this black void was the infinite itself: their dreams are outlined and occur against a background of immutable ebony. No cries, no convulsions, nothing but the rigidity of a face full of thought. Since the gods were gone and the Christ had not yet come, there was, from the time of Cicero to that of Marcus Aurelius, a unique moment when man was completely alone.

Centuries before Cicero and Marcus Aurelius the poet Pindar wrote in his Eighth *Pythian Ode*:

> Short is the space of time in which the happiness of mortal men grows up, and even so it falls to the ground, when struck down by adverse doom. Creatures of a day, what is any one? what is he not? Man is but a dream of a shadow. . . .

During this same period, Aeschylus cited the transitoriness of man's actions in reference to "the oar-blade's fading footprint" as the Greeks sailed for Troy [*Agamemnon,* line 695]; and he has Agamemnon himself on his return home remark only a little while before his death: ". . . and yet time has buried in the mounding sand the sea cables since that day when against Ilium the army and the ships put to sea" [*Ibid.,* lines 983-87]. Orestes, in *The Eumenides,* says that "Time in his aging course destroys all things" [line 286]. In like manner, Sophocles writes that "great Time withers all things" [*Ajax,* line 713]; and from Sophocles' lost play called *Achilles' Loves* a simile has come down to us likening love to a piece of ice held in the hand of a child. Thus the relentless force of time and the ephemeral nature of man and of man's desiring obtained vivid expression in the greatest of the ancient Greek lyric poets and writers of tragedy.

In the period specifically mentioned by Flaubert — the period from Cicero to Marcus Aurelius — there is a remarkable concern with time. We have seen already from the *De Rerum Natura* certain verses of Lucretius on the subject, and one can cite from the same poem others as memorable; for example, Lucretius' discussion of "the gate of death for things" ["rebus . . . ianua leti"] and the following passages:

> . . . all things gradually decay, and go to the tomb outworn by the ancient lapse of years [II. 1173-74].

> Again, do you not see that even stones are overcome by time, that tall turrets fall and rocks decay, that the gods' temples and their images wear out and crack, nor can their holy divinity . . . strive against nature's laws? . . . Into what place have so many deeds of men so often fallen. . . .? . . . . The door of death . . . is not closed for the heavens, nor for sun and earth and the deep waters of the sea, but stands open and awaits them with its vast and monstrous mouth. [V. 306-75, *passim.*]

> For time changes the nature of the whole universe, and one state of things must pass into another, and nothing remains as it was. . . . [V. 828-30].

> So rolling time [*volvenda aetas*] changes the seasons of things [V. 1276].

With Horace there is a melancholy expression of time's swift passing, in verses of such beauty and pertinence to the lot of man that they give us still the name of one of the most famous lyric motifs in western letters: the motif of *carpe diem* [pluck the day], in which the day is often changed *(carpe rosam)* to a rose. The famous passage occurs in one of Horace's best-known poems — the eleventh in the first book of *Odes* — the lyric to Leuconoë that ends: ". . . be wise, strain your wines, and since the space of life is short, cut down your hopes. Even as we speak, envious time has fled away. Pluck today, trusting as little as possible in tomorrow." ["Carpe diem, quam minimum credula postero."] The beauty and irony of this old motif have persisted over the centuries in many poems in many languages, and John Addington Symonds has written on the subject an essay, "On the Pathos of the Rose in Poetry," which traces in classical letters and in the poetry of England, France and Italy, the theme of the rose as a symbol of maidenhood and of youth that passes like a flower.

Depiction of the relentless passing of time [*ferox aetas*] is a kind of *leitmotif* in Horaces's *Odes*; and we hear it in them again and again in relation to the lot of man:

> Eheu fugaces, Postume, Postume,
> labuntur anni.... [II. xiv. 1-2]

"Alas, O Postumus, Postumus, the swift years are gliding away, nor will pious virtue give pause to wrinkles, to advancing age, or to invincible death. . . ." Thus, in the life of man, "day treads upon the heel of day, and new moons go on waning. . . ." [II. xviii. 15-16]. Horace asks, "What does injurious time not ruin?" [III. vi. 45]; and for man he sees this as the end: ". . . the swiftly changing moons repair their losses in the sky. But we, when we have descended where righteous Aeneas and rich Tullus and Ancus have gone, are dust and shadow" ["pulvis et ombra sumus"] (IV. vii. 13-15).

Before Horace, Catullus, the most youthfully impassioned of the great Latin poets, had written similarly of man's lot in verses urging his Lesbia to love him while there was yet time: "Suns can go down and rise again: but once our brief light has set, the night

is everlasting in one long sleep" ["Nox est perpetua una dor-
mienda"] (V. 4-6).

For Tibullus, a contemporary of Horace, "How quickly youth
is gone! And the day does not stand idle or return. . . . Cruel gods!
the snake sheds its years and is new: but Fate gives no respite to
beauty" [I. iv. 27-28; 35-36]. — "Use your life while it is still in
its flowering spring. Its foot is swift as it glides away" [I. viii.
47-48].

In the second century of the Christian era, Marcus Aurelius,
writing his *Meditations* in Greek, brings us for all his Stoicism a
further sense of what Flaubert meant by the "more profound"
melancholy of antiquity. Like Horace, Marcus Aurelius writes of
time in words men still remember; and I cite him here from the
anonymous translation in which I first met him many years ago:

> Flux and change are forever renewing the universe; just as
> the unbroken course of time makes the infinity of ages
> ever young.

> In this stream, then, wherein there is no abiding, what is
> there among the multitude of things that go swimming past,
> on which a man shall set his heart? It is but as if a child
> should fall in love with the sparrow flitting over his head;
> and ere his love be well begun, the bird is out of sight.
> [VI. 15]

For Marcus Aurelius, "Time is a rushing torrent, a stream fed by
life and its changes. One thing swims into sight and is swept away,
another comes fleeting past, and a third will anon be here to take
its place" [IV. 43]. Though the *Meditations* advise man to "traverse . . . [his] little moment of time at peace with Nature, and
reach [his] journey's end in all content, as an olive that ripens
and falls" [IV. 48], one senses the pertinence of Flaubert's remark
on the "background of immutable ebony" in such words as the
following: "How speedily shall time hide all things in darkness!
How many it has hidden already! . . . . In a little while . . . the
memory of all things is swallowed up in eternity" [VI. 58; VII. 10].

In Marcus Aurelius we even find the *ubi sunt* motif that we
shall consider later in the mediaeval period:

> Where are the great wits of old: the great peerers into the
> future? the classic examples of arrogance? Where are Charax,
> Demetrius the Platonist, Eudaemon. . . .? All were creatures
> of a day; all have been dead these many years. [VIII. 25]

By the time of Saint Augustine (354-430) the influence of
Christ had come and with it the development of Christian thought;
and Augustine's discussions of time show man with a sense of his
being part of eternity — beyond the reach of time through "spiritual
contact with the unchangeable Light" of his God. Even in this
earthly life, according to Augustine, "to some it has been granted
by a certain holy inebriation of mind [sancta quadem ebrietate . . .
mentis], alienated from fleeting temporal things below, to gaze on
the eternal light of Wisdom."

Augustine in his humanity was able to write very memorable
words on the ephemeral nature of man in "this our house of grass":
"Space presents us things to love, time removes the things we
love; and leaves the soul crowds of phantoms. . . ." Yet, with the
Christian dimension of his thought, Augustine saw more to life than
Horace or Marcus Aurelius saw, and he proclaimed men's obliga-
tion "to stand alone and single . . . severed from the multitude and
crowd of things born and decaying, lovers of eternity and of unity,
if we desire to cleave to our One God and Lord." As for the eternal
Light, "he that knows . . . what that Light is . . . knows eternity.
Love knows it."

Augustine writes of his infinite God in terms of space: "So
also did I endeavour to conceive of thee, Life of my life, as vast
through infinite spaces, on every side penetrating the whole mass
of the universe and beyond it, every way, through unmeasurable
boundless spaces. . . ." Here the parallel with Lucretius' thought is
almost as fascinating as Augustine's divergence from it; but the
passage shows the vast difference in conception between the materialist and Christian views of space and time. The Christian
Augustine writes of his God: "Thine is the day and thine the night;
at thy beckoning the moments pass swiftly by." ["Tuus est dies et
tua est nox; ad nutum tuum momenta transvolant."] And Augustine
notes that *today* for God is Eternity.

In Saint Augustine we find one of the great spiritual geniuses
of the West, and his insights represent an aspect of mystical intui-

tion that recurs with such figures as St. Gregory the Great (c. 540-604) and later in the middle ages with St. Bernard (1090-1153).

* * *

In both the sacred and secular literature of the European middle ages one comes upon the recurrent theme of time that engulfs all human strength and loveliness and grandeur and genius and all earthly glory, though the theme often occurs obliquely, as in the famous motif of *ubi sunt* (which we have seen already in Marcus Aurelius), where the emphasis is characteristically more on the effects of time than on time itself. Etienne Gilson has traced this motif back to Isaiah [33.18]:

> Thine heart shall meditate terror.
> Where is the scribe? where is the receiver,
> where is he that counted the towers?

Gilson shows the motif also in Baruch [3.16-19] and in I Corinthians [I. 19-20] and cites examples from Greece and Rome, from Arabic, from Greek, Latin and Syriac patrologies, and from numerous mediaeval and later poets and theologians. But the most famous and the most beautiful of them all is the "Ballade des dames du temps jadis" of François Villon:

> Tell me where, or in what land
> Is Flora, the lovely Roman lady,
> Archipiada, or Thaïs
> Who was her cousin-german.
> Echo, speaking when one calls
> Over the river or over the pool,
> Whose beauty was much more than human.
> But where are the snows of yesteryear?. . . .

> [Dictes moy ou, n'en quel pays,
> Est Flora la belle Rommaine,
> Archipiades, ne Thaïs,
> Qui fut sa cousine germaine,
> Echo parlant quant bruyt on maine
> Dessus riviere ou sus estan,
> Qui beaulté ot trop plus qu'humaine.
> Mais ou sont les neiges d'antan?. . . .]

The musical verses with their rhythms from the greatest poet of mediaeval France bring name after name before us. And with the music and the rhythm of Villon's words the old names come only to vanish away again like melting layer after layer of snows of other years, and the marvellous refrain ("Mais ou sont les neiges d'antan?") presides over it all, as if in an ancient ritual on the swift and final passing of woman's loveliness.

The Renaissance brought great changes into European literature, and during the sixteenth and seventeenth centuries time seems to have come to play characteristically a more direct role in significant poetry than it had played in the middle ages. During these years the *carpe diem* theme of Horace tended to replace the theme of *ubi sunt* in popularity; and here the verses of Ronsard in France and those of Herrick and Marvell in England are among the most memorable in their treatment of time.

Ronsard, in his poems to Cassandra and Marie and Helen, wrote some of the best-known rose poems in the modern world — as famous as Herrick's "Gather ye rose-buds while ye may, / Old Time is still a-flying. ..." In Ronsard, formal elegance does not conceal the underlying sadness in the poems. One may cite in point the most famous of the odes to Cassandra Salviati, in which Ronsard invites his mistress to go at evening to see the rose which had opened only that morning its crimson dress to the sun.

> Alas! See in how short a while,
> Mignonne, it has upon the ground,
> Alas! alas! let fall its beauties!
> ... ...
>
> Then, if you listen to me, Mignonne,
> While your age flowers
> In its most fresh newness,
> Pluck, pluck your youth:
> As it fades this flower
> Old age will make your beauty fade.

So subtly has Ronsard's mood of sadness penetrated the verbal music of his poem that one can hear as he reads in the French four echoes from the word *alas!:*

> Las! Voyez comme en peu d'espace,
> Mignonne, elle a, dessus la place,
> Las! las! ses beautés laissé choir!. . . .

And the concluding admonition ("Cueillez, cueillez votre jeunesse. . . ." — "Pluck, pluck your youth [like a flower] . . . .") is Horace's *carpe diem* — one of mankind's ageless answers to the ravages of Time.

Ronsard knew the sombre reality beyond this stress on the present moment; and he writes in darker verses:

> Le temps s'en va, le temps s'en va, ma Dame;
> Las! le temps non, mais nous nous en allons. . . .

> [Time goes away, time goes away, my Lady;
> Alas! time no, but we do go. . . .]

If Ronsard thus gave to France her finest verses on the motif of *carpe diem,* one must still turn to English poetry and Andrew Marvell for the most powerful use of the theme. In the poem "To His Coy Mistress" Marvell provides several unforgettable and contrasting images of time. He tells his mistress that, under other circumstances, he would have waited all but endlessly for her love. . . .

> But at my back I always hear
> Time's wingèd chariot hurrying near:
> And yonder all before us lie
> Deserts of vast eternity. . . .

Here the rhythm and sound of the verses enhance the strange and desolate images of Time's wingèd chariot and the deserts of eternity. The poem employs also a powerfully ironic vocabulary in building up contrasts between coyness and desire against a background of human mortality and, by a reference to Time's "slow-chapt power," presents Time under the grim image of an animal with inexorable jaws that grind mankind to death.

Earlier in the century, in 1609, there had appeared the first edition of Shakespeare's sonnets, which show a great poet's remarkable preoccupation with time. Here "wasteful," "swift-footed," and "devouring" Time is "never-resting" with his dreadful scythe or crooked knife and awesome sickle-hour. He is a "bloody tyrant" who changes the day of youth to "sullied night," carves with his hours on beauty's brow, smears over gravestones, and finally at the last for the living puts his cruel hand to his scythe. Worst of all, the poet knows "that Time will come and take my love away."

One sonnet (106) begins:

> When in the chronicle of wasted time
> I see descriptions of the fairest wights. . . .

And another (Sonnet 60):

> Like as the waves make towards the pebbled shore,
> So do our minutes hasten to their end. . . .

Sonnet 65 recalls Lucretius' "door of death" in its sombre catalogue of all that time devours:

> Since brass, nor stone, nor earth, nor boundless sea,
> But sad mortality o'ersways their power,
> How with this rage shall beauty hold a plea,
> Whose action is no stronger than a flower?
>
> O, how shall summer's honey breath hold out
> Against the wreckful siege of battering days,
> When rocks impregnable are not so stout,
> Nor gates of steel so strong, but Time decays?

In Sonnet 12 we even seem to hear in the opening verse the sound of a great clock ticking:

> When I do count the clock that tells the time,
> And see the brave day sunk in hideous night. . . .

In Shakespeare's sonnets there is for man no mitigating vision of eternity, so that Time ultimately seems here once more as dark as Flaubert's ebony. But this is to change with other great writers of the age.

In a way the seventeenth century can be seen in significant European literature as the century of eternity. It was an age of great prose, and many of the finest prose writers were pulpit orators. In France, during this period, Bossuet reminds us that "there is never more than an instant between us and nothingness"; but his Christian view of life concerns eternity. In England, Jeremy Taylor writes of an ephemeral rose, at first almost with the accent of a Ronsard; but there is no admonition at the last to pluck the flower, and the conclusion looks another way. The passage is a famous one in English prose:

> .... But so have I seen a Rose newly springing from the clefts of its hood, and at first it was fair as the Morning, and full with the dew of Heaven, as a Lambs fleece; but when a ruder breath had forced open its virgin modesty and dismantled its too youthful and unripe retirements, it began to put on darknesse, and to decline to softnesse, and the symptomes of a sickly age; it bowed the head, and broke its stalk, and at night having lost some of its leaves, and all its beauty, it fell into the portion of weeds and outworn faces. . . .
> . . . So does the fairest beauty change, and it will be as bad with you and me; and then, what servants shall we have to wait upon us in the grave, what friends to visit us, what officious people to cleanse away the moist and unwholsom cloud reflected upon our faces from the sides of the weeping vaults, which are the longest weepers for our funeral. . . . A man may read a sermon, the best and most passionate that ever men preached, if he shall but enter into the sepulchres of Kings. [*Holy Dying* (1651)]

There is always in such writings as these the assumption of a further dimension for mankind beyond time. "Our life is but short," says Robert Burton in *The Anatomy of Melancholy,* "a very dream, and while we look about, *immortalitas adest,* eternity is at hand. . . ." From these years also Sir Thomas Browne affords us memorable passages on time and timelessness in Christian thought. In Browne's words "Time . . . antiquates Antiquities and hath an art to make dust of all things" [*Hydriotaphia*]. There is no antidote against time's Opium, for Time "makes the Pyramids pillars of snow, and all that's past a moment." But in the *Religio Medici* Browne comments on the Christian mystery of Time in relation to a passage we have cited earlier:

> *Before Abraham was, I am,* is the saying of Christ; yet it is true in some sense, if I say it myself; for I was not only before my self, but Adam, that is, in the Idea of

God, and the decree of that Synod held from all Eternity.
And in this sense, I say, the World was before the Creation, and at an end before it had a beginning; and thus
was I dead before I was alive: though my grave be England, my dying place was Paradise; and Eve miscarried
of me before she conceiv'd of Cain.

From this century, too, comes Vaughan's poem "The World" with
its mystical image of what lies above or beyond time:

> I saw Eternity the other night
> Like a great *Ring* of pure and endless light,
>   All calm as it was bright,
> And round beneath it, Time in hours, days, years
>   Driven by the spheres
> Like a vast shadow mov'd, in which the world
>   And all her train were hurl'd. . . .

One learns at the last that the great ring of Eternity is provided
by the mystical Bridegroom for his bride. Thus the Christian vision
entails beyond time for man a sense of the bright radiance of
Eternity — such a vision as Dante furnished at the end of the
Paradiso when the middle ages were drawing to a close.

* * *

It is of interest to consider the changing character of human
thought and feeling from age to age within a relatively narrow
cultural radius. On so constant and pressing a matter as time there
naturally persist recurrent attitudes in literature; but representative
works of different periods reflect characteristic changes even here.
One would not make much sense, for example, in calling the
eighteenth century in western Europe "the century of eternity."

Baudelaire once wrote of Voltaire that, "like all lazy beings,
[he] hated mystery"; and it may seem somewhat surprising to find
Voltaire, in *The Good Brahman*, writing about the mystery of time
in words that echo both Augustine and Pascal:

> I have been born, I live in time, and I do not know
> what time is. I find myself in a spot between two ex-
> tremities, as our wise men say, and I have no idea of
> eternity.

But if the problem posed is the same as Augustine's and Pascal's, there appears to be no very serious spiritual longing in the good Brahman — and this would seem to reflect rather clearly also the attitude of Voltaire.

In the eighteenth century another remarkably imaginative literary intelligence was concerned with recapturing the past time of history. This was Edward Gibbon who, in his *Autobiography,* recounts for us the almost visionary inspiration that lay behind his great *History of the Decline and Fall of the Roman Empire:*

> It was at Rome on the 15th of October, 1764, as I sat musing amidst the ruins of the Capitol, while the barefooted friars were singing vespers in the Temple of Jupiter, that the idea of writing the decline and fall of the city first started to my mind.

It was only later that Gibbon decided to write the decline and fall of the whole Empire; but the description here of his first inspiration is of special interest. An anonymous reviewer in the *Times Literary Supplement* some years ago had this to say of it:

> In the facets of that single sentence [Gibbon] catches every necessary ingredient in his tremendous theme: the physical evidence of the past in the ruined remains; the representatives of the historical force which changed the world and survives, in the chanting friars. And where does the musing historian make them chant? Not in the Church of Santa Maria di Ara Coeli, nor (which would be the same thing) 'where the Temple of Jupiter used to stand,' for not a trace of the temple remains above ground; but with the historian's second sight and the practiced writer's second simplicity, *in* the Temple of Jupiter. Perhaps there was poetic licence, for the moment is poetic. The past is merged with the present.

In a sense this is analogous to Proust's famous half-visionary experience with his *madeleine.* And the great historian, like the great novelist, managed under such inspiration to win, as it were, for a little while a partial victory over time.

*   *   *

One may find in France a bridge on the theme of Time between the eighteenth century and Romanticism in Antoine-Léonard Thomas' neo-classical "Ode on Time" and "The Lake" of Lamartine. The Romantic poet uses key phrases ("the ocean of the ages" and "O Time, suspend your flight") that are found in the earlier poem; but he invests them with a new lyricism and an entirely new emotion in verses that are among the most famous in the French language. In "The Lake" Lamartine uses a central image of the eternal flux of things and of time and has his love cry out to Time to stop its flight at the height of their joy. But Time, as in the mediaeval dawn-songs or *aubades* and as in *Romeo and Juliet* and in all such moments of lovers' happiness, pays no heed:

> "O time, suspend your flight! and you, happy hours,
>   Suspend your course!
> Let us enjoy the swift delights
>   Of the fairest of our days!
> ... ...
>
> "But I ask in vain some moments still,
>   Time escapes me and flees away;
> ... ... and the dawn
>   Comes to end the night."

With De Quincey and later with Baudelaire, under the influence of opium or hashish, time moves at a different pace. De Quincey tells us in rather macabre fashion in his *Confessions of an English Opium Eater* that, in opium dreams, he lived "thousands of years ... and was buried in stone coffins, with mummies and sphinxes, in narrow chambers at the heart of eternal pyramids."

Baudelaire, in "The Poem of Hashish," a part of his book called *The Artificial Paradises,* proclaims man's enjoyment now and then of privileged moments in which he experiences vast new perspectives, and he cites man's attempt also on occasion "to create paradise by pharmacy." The effect of hashish includes what Baudelaire calls "moral hallucination" (e.g., the belief that one has become God), and he terms the drug "a perfect instrument of Satan." Under its influence time and space expand monstrously, and in the state known to Orientals as *kief* suffering and the idea of time disappear, or appear transfigured or, at least, as if invested with a sort of poetic melancholy. But the will is weakened, so that

use of the drug constitutes a slow suicide; and Baudelaire observes
that "in fact, every man who does not accept the conditions of life
sells his soul."

Yet Baudelaire took both opium and hashish, probably in great
part to escape momentarily from the terrible *spleen* or *ennui* that
pursued him in life. We find this depicted in the poems of *Les
Fleurs du Mal*; and this boredom is often evident in Baudelaire's
horror of time itself, which is a recurrent subject in his work.

In the part of his journal called, from a suggestion in Poe, *My
Heart Laid Bare,* Baudelaire writes: "At every moment we are
crushed by the idea and the sensation of time." One finds further
evidence of this in the poem "L'Horloge" ("The Clock"), in which
Baudelaire is preoccupied with time in a way that recalls Shakespeare in the Sonnets some 250 years before. Baudelaire's imagery
here is strange and memorable.

> Horloge! dieu sinistre, effrayant, impassible. . . .
>
> O Clock! sinister, terrifying, impassive god
> Whose finger threatens. . . .
> ... ...
> Three thousand six hundred times an hour the Second
> Whispers: *Remember!* —Swift, with its
> Insect voice, the Present says: I am the Past,
> And have drained your life with my obscene tube.
> *Remember! Souviens-toi!* prodigal! *Esto memor!*
> (My metal throat speaks every tongue.)
> ... ...
> The day declines; night comes on; *remember!*
> The gulf is always thirsty; the water-clock runs dry. . . .

And the poem closes with the remark that soon the hour of death
will come and it will be too late even to repent.

In a prose poem, also called "The Clock" and which he terms
a pretentious bit of *galanterie,* Baudelaire notes that the Chinese
tell time by cats' eyes. And he writes that, if he leans towards his
cat (or his mistress — one cannot distinguish between them here),
"whether by night or day in the full daylight or deep shadow, in
the depths of her adorable eyes I always see the hour clearly,
always the same, one vast, solemn hour, as great as space itself,
without divisions into minutes or seconds — a motionless hour not
indicated on the clocks. . . ." And if anyone interrupted his gaze

to ask what he was seeking and whether he saw the time in those eyes, he would answer at once without hesitation: "Yes, I see the hour; it is eternity!"

Baudelaire had a clear sense of the difference between time and eternity. His friend Théophile Gautier had written in a famous poem called "L'Art" that . . .

> Everything passes away. —Robust art
> Alone has eternity.

But Baudelaire knew that even the finest art has an end in time; and he expressed this most clearly in the last stanza of "Les Phares" ("The Lighthouses"), a poem in which he sees works of art as man's best testimony to human worth, but still time-bound, this side of eternity:

> For truly, Lord, the best witness
> That we can give of our worth
> Is this burning sob that rolls from age to age
> And comes to die at the edge of your eternity!

A little later in the century Rimbaud will write that Eternity is recovered:

> It is the sea gone
> With the sun. ("L'Eternité.")

* * *

In our present age many gifted writers in the West have lost the sense of eternity. Yet some of our finest literature shows a peculiar preoccupation with time that seems to reflect an instinctive human longing for immortality. Now at the last I shall try to suggest a few of the more memorable attitudes towards time in important and representative novelists of our century. I shall concentrate for the most part upon statements by the authors themselves and draw largely for my examples from the writings of Proust, Hemingway, Wolfe, and Joyce.

In *A la recherche du temps perdu (Remembrance of Things Past)*, Proust's novel of Time and Memory, Time is Proust's great protagonist — Time set within a musical structure. His book begins with an overture, in which most of the main characters are introduced. One is not likely to forget the opening lines: "For a long time I used to go to bed early. Sometimes, when I had put out my candle, my eyes would close so quickly that I had not even time to say 'I'm going to sleep.' " A little further on, the style develops a half-mystical aura as Proust writes of the passing of Time: "When a man is asleep, he has in a circle round him the chain of the hours, the sequence of the years, the order of the heavenly host. . . ." And the passage thereafter continues: "It always happened that when I awoke like this, and my mind struggled in an unsuccessful attempt to discover where I was, everything would be moving round me through the darkness: things, places, years."

Hundreds of pages later, the end of *Swann's Way* shows Proust's musical thematic structure in his discussion of Time; and the last part of the whole work, *The Past Recaptured,* concludes with a memorable passage: "If, at least, there were granted me time enough to complete my work, I would . . . therein describe men . . . as occupying in Time a place far more considerable than the so restricted one allotted them in space, a place, on the contrary, extending boundlessly since, giant-like, reaching far back into the years, they touch simultaneously epochs of their lives — with countless intervening days between — so widely separated from one another in Time."

D. H. Lawrence, who made a mystery of the blood, called the present instant our *terra incognita,* "one great mystery of Time"; and he wrote of it: "The quivering nimble hour of the present, this is the quick of Time. This is the immanence. The quick of the universe is the *pulsating, carnal self,* mysterious and palpable. So it is always."

Of modern writers few have had so remarkable a gift as Hemingway for representing concretely this sort of immediate sensation, as may be seen in the brilliant use of the present participle in the following passage from *Green Hills of Africa*:

> . . . me sitting, the butt of my rifle on my foot, the barrel in the crook of my left arm, a flask of whiskey between my knees, pouring the whiskey into a tin cup and passing it over my shoulder in the dark for M'Cola

to pour water into it from the canteen, drinking this the
first one of the day, the finest one there is, and looking
at the thick bush we passed in the dark, feeling the cool
wind of night and smelling the good smell of Africa. . . .

This "quick of Time" that is all men's lot, set against the two
billion light years probed now by our great astronomical cameras
and telescopes, affords a haunting irony to the human situation.

Thomas Wolfe, who shared some of the Proustian concepts,
differed from Proust, among other matters, in his large concern
for an imaginative projection of Time beyond the memory of the
race of men. He writes in *The Making of a Novel* of three time
elements inherent in his material — the actual present, the past,
and what he conceived to be "time immutable, the time of rivers,
mountains, oceans, and the earth; a kind of eternal and unchanging
universe of time against which would be projected the transience
of man's life, the bitter briefness of his day." In sleep Wolfe's mind
and memory "blazed with a fiery river of unending images: the
whole vast reservoirs of memory. . . ." And yet — "From above
that universe of dreams there shone forever a tranquil, muted and
unchanging light of time."

It remained for James Joyce to treat in fiction ultimately a
timeless world. In *A Portrait of the Artist as a Young Man,* in the
famous hell-fire sermons, Joyce had treated the idea of an eternity
of punishment. In *Ulysses* he introduces a beautiful dance of the
hours, and the element of time itself seems in this novel on occasion
as surrealistic as the watches in Dali's *Persistence of Memory.*
Here, too, occurs the following passage — mysterious, timeless, cast
amidst men's wanderings and love and life and death, and the
wandering of the planets and the sun, and the rising and the falling
of the moon and the great sea. It is an eerie passage, unlike any
other that I know in any literature:

> Shouldering their bags they trudged, the red Egyptians.
> His blued feet out of turnedup trousers slapped the clammy
> sand. . . With woman steps she followed: the ruffian and
> his strolling mort. . . . Passing now. . . . Across the sands
> of all the world, followed by the sun's flaming sword, to
> the west, trekking to evening lands. She trudges, schlepps,
> trains, drags, trascines her load. A tide westering moon-
> drawn, in her wake. Tides, myriadislanded, within her,

blood not mine, *oinopa ponton,* a winedark sea. Behold
the handmaid of the moon. In sleep the wet sign calls her
hour, bids her rise. Bridebed, childbed, bed of death,
ghostcandled. *Omnis caro ad te veniet.* He comes, pale
vampire. . . . His lips lipped and mouthed fleshless lips of
air: mouth to her womb. Oomb, allwombing tomb. His
mouth moulded issuing breath, unspeeched: ooeeehah:
roar of cataract planets, globed, blazing, roaring waya-
wayawayawayawayaway.

Finally, in *Finnegans Wake,* we have the ultimate, timeless,
unique world of Joyce's creation — in which myth and legend and
history meet on equal terms with immediate, contemporary life;
with fragments of popular songs, old saws, slogans, quotations;
and with gods and heroes of many ages and many lands. Joyce's
strange lyricism recurs in a myriad changing forms, and the motif
of timeless Time is an important part of the incredibly complex
patterns in words and narrative. The story of the Fall — the Fall
of Adam, of Everyman-Finnegan, of Lucifer, of Rome, of the
sun, of the Stock Market in Wall Street, of Humpty Dumpty, of
Newton's apple — echoes and reechoes throughout the book; and
one important element in narrative structure relates to Vico's ("Old
Vico Roundpoint's") theory of cycles: "The Vico road goes round
and round to meet where terms begin." The book itself begins in
the middle of a sentence and ends the same way, so that in a
circular motion it ends in its beginning and so goes on forever.

A few phrases from *Finnegans Wake* will suggest the versatile
word-play and the variety of tone and subject in Joyce's references
to what he called, as we have seen earlier, "seeking spoor through
the deep timefield": "Per omnibus secular seekalarum" . . . "when
yea, he hath no mananas" . . . "Thyme, that chef of seasoners" . . .
"Dark ages clasp the daisy roots" . . . "nuncandtunc and for
simper" . . . "Tick up on time. Howday you doom?"

Beyond the gay humor and the nearly Rabelaisian gusto that
recur in Joyce there is thus recurrent also a note of ultimate sadness,
as in his reference to "Mark Time's Finist Joke. Putting Allspace
in a Notshall" — or in the following expression of human bewilder-
ment before man's helpless situation in Time: "In the buginning
is the woid, in the muddle is the sound-dance and thereinofter
you're in the unbewised again. . . ."

And so at the last with Joyce, as with Proust and Wolfe and Lawrence and Hemingway, there is no transcendent vision to link man spiritually with eternity.

* * *

In our consideration of Time this evening we have seen how man over the centuries has recognized Time's remorseless power, its transience, and its mystery: "Thyme, that chef of seasoners." The irony of "the oar-blade's fading foot-print" is one with the irony of the fading rose and the vanished snows or beautiful ladies of other years. Time may come with his scythe in his dread sickle-hour or in a wingèd chariot — or men may see him in the waves hastening to the shore, or hear his warning voice each hour in the 3600 tickings of the clock. Or he may appear in all his "slow-chapt power," inexorably grinding life away, just as he wears out gates of steel and "makes the pyramids pillars of snow." Thus, with Time's passing, man sees himself as dust and ashes and looks with lonely envy upon the sun and moon that set and rise again, while mortal man must sleep forever.

Christian thought and faith transcend all this in the individual soul's ultimate, immortal relationship with God. But one finds, as we have seen, in the perspective of many modern minds no such conception of personal eternity. In the expression of such minds one has even at times a sense of the recurrence of Flaubert's "melancholy of antiquity" with its unrelieved black void, waiting beyond what is often called today the "absurdity" of life.

Yet men yearn as much as ever, with Augustine, "to arrive at some spiritual contact with the unchangeable Light." Those who fail in their search or who lack faith in the Light's existence or in the possibility of union with It must always sound a lonely note in their furthest considerations of Time. But, in Augustine's words, Love knows that Light, and "he that knows . . . what that Light is . . . knows Eternity."

DATE DUE	
~~NOV 07 1989~~	
~~FEB 07 1991~~	
~~JUL 03 1991~~	